THE LIFE OF THE
WOLF

THE LIFE OF THE
WOLF

Aimee Clark

METRO BOOKS
New York

METRO BOOKS
New York

An Imprint of Sterling Publishing Co., Inc.
1166 Avenue of the Americas
New York, NY 10036

METRO BOOKS and the distinctive Metro Books logo are registered trademarks of
Sterling Publishing Co., Inc.

© 2018 Regency House Publishing Limited

ISBN 978-1-4351-6871-8

For information about custom editions, special sales, and premium and corporate
purchases, please contact Sterling Special Sales at 800-805-5489 or
specialsales@sterlingpublishing.com.

Manufactured in China

2 4 6 8 10 9 7 5 3 1

sterlingpublishing.com

CONTENTS

INTRODUCTION

INTRODUCTION

Few creatures have captured the imagination of mankind more than the wolf. Depicted in prehistoric cave paintings and modern films alike, this cousin of man's best friend seems mysterious, intriguing, and more than a little dangerous. From their earliest stages of evolution throughout their long and tumultuous history, these apex predators continue to fascinate.

As writer and environmentalist Henry David Thoreau once said, "*The story of Romulus and Remus being suckled by a wolf is not a meaningless fable.*" In fact, this mythological story of how the founders of Rome came to be, shows the bond between mankind and wolves. This fable is one of the few stories involving the wolf where the animal was not seen as the villain. Other positive stories of the wolf stem from Native American culture.

Nearly every tribe of indigenous Americans has its own version of the wolf as a god and/or part of the tribe. Generally considered a being of healing, the wolf was associated with strength, courage, and loyalty in Native American culture. Considered to be closely related to humans by many tribes, some even tell stories of their first ancestors being transformed from wolves into men. In Shoshone legend, *Wolf* is the noble creator god, while Anishinabe mythology shows the wolf as the brother and best friend of their culture's most renowned hero.

ABOVE: In Norse mythology Fenrir is one of three malevolent wolves. He was the eldest son of Loki and Angerboda.

LEFT: A sculpture by Giovanni Ceccarini depicting the founding of Rome. A she-wolf is feeding Romulus and Remus. The sculpture is situated in the Piazza del Popolo in Rome.

RIGHT & OVERLEAF: The Eurasian gray wolf.

powerful than fact, and consequently, this fear has prevailed throughout much of history.

Misunderstandings of the nature of these creatures has often led to fear, anger, and persecution. Humanity has often seen wolves as dangerous predators that encroach upon their space and threaten their way of life. The facts support the concept that wolves may very well say the same about humanity.

The constant spread of civilization into more and more remote areas led to the destruction of habitats for many top predators, not just for wolves. For the wolf though, this encroachment onto their territories by man with their livestock and other domesticated species, led to wolves becoming a particular target for destruction. Livestock safety took precedent over the lives of wild animals in the minds of most colonizing Americans. Further reduction in the populations of the wolf's natural prey, through hunting and habitat destruction, exacerbated these conflicts between man and beast.

Like people, wolves live in familial communities called packs, where every member serves a vital role. These packs have a structure much like that of humans: they have male and female pairings, with a dominant pair ruling over the entire group. The pack works as a group to protect the young and the old of the group and other extended

However, these positive connections between humanity and the wolf were pushed to the background by the advancement of civilization. Much of the comradery felt between people and wolves was forgotten as man's push into the wolf's natural habitat brought these noble animals into violent conflict with the people who once honored them. This shift in sentiment is evident via the change in the wolf's position within mythologies and fables.

The fairy story *Little Red Riding Hood* is known for its dedicated granddaughter and vicious wolf. This wolf was no friend of humanity and epitomized the fear of the many who believed that wolves would happily kill and eat a human. The fact is that wolves rarely attack people and only when provoked. However, misconception is more

ABOVE: A helmet and collar crafted in the shape of a wolf's head. Made from wood and shell by the Tlingit indigenous people from the northwest American Pacific coast, it dates from the 18th century.

RIGHT: The eerie sound of the wolf howling is legendary. Their favorite time to howl is between 7:00PM and midnight.

family members including aunts, uncles, cousins, etc. Similarities between wolf and human families are often overlooked and are rarely appreciated.

Unlike humans, wolves are largely a nomadic species. While they generally stay within their own territories, those territories can often stretch for hundreds of miles. If the weather, habitat, or other conditions become less hospitable, wolf packs are adapted to relocate to other areas that will provide them with better conditions for their survival. These moves also allow for the repopulation of food sources and help wolves avoid overcrowding within their own species. Thus, it is not surprising that wolves can be very protective of their territories.

Struggling for space with human beings was not the only factor in the wolf's decline. Fighting with other packs over territory slowed

ABOVE: A small pack of three eastern timber wolves gather on a rocky slope in the North American wilderness.

OVERLEAF: The social structure of the wolf pack is complicated and changes from year to year. Wolf packs have a clear "pecking order" or hierarchy. A younger wolf lower down in the pecking order may challenge an alpha wolf for pack leadership. If the alpha wolf loses this challenge, the younger wolf will take over the pack and the older wolf with leave the pack, find another mate, and even start a new pack.

their growth as a species. Today, evolution has ensured that packs command smaller territories and interact less violently should another pack arrive on its territory.

The wolf is one of the few species that man has deliberately tried to drive to extinction. Over a few hundred years, human interference has caused the decline of many species, but this has been more accidental than deliberate. For example, the dodo bird was hunted to extinction by sailors who arrived in Mauritius in the 17th century. Yet at the time, they were unaware that they were wiping out an entire species. Wolf hunters, however, knew that this was exactly what they were doing.

The prolific nature of the wild wolf made this extermination effort truly impressive in a terrible way. With wolves existing in every area, climate, and ecosystem around the world, only a concerted effort on the part of mankind could create the kind of mass persecution wolves once faced worldwide.

While there are only two species of wolf —the gray wolf and the red wolf —there are dozens of subspecies associated with each of the two. Several of the subspecies have already gone extinct, never to be encountered again except in old records and books. Others, such as the Ethiopian wolf, currently on the critically endangered list, are rapidly moving towards the same fate. However, more positive and proactive conservation efforts have meant that some subspecies have made it off the list altogether.

It has only been man's interference that has led to the disasterous decline in wolf numbers around the world. Today, they now exist in just a few pockets in relatively few countries. As Canadian writer and environmentalist Farley Mowat once said, *"We have doomed the wolf not for what it is, but for what we deliberately and mistakenly perceived it to be..."*

Fortunately, our understanding of this rare and enigmatic species has increased enormously over the past few decades and it is hoped that wolf numbers can grow, so the trend towards extinction can be stopped. Today, the cloud of uncertainty and fear that surround wolves has been lifted and it is now widely understood that there can be a successful coexistence between mankind and wolves. Through social and legal avenues, the plight of the wolf is now taking center stage. Laws have been designed to protect the wolf, and conservation efforts have led the charge for returning this keystone species to every corner of the world. Humanity is the determining factor as to whether wolves will survive and thrive or go the way of the dodo, the woolly mammoth, and the saber-toothed tiger to extinction.

Besides being notable for their beauty, intelligence, and prowess, wolves are particularly infamous for their mysterious howling that can fill the night air with spooky echoes that chill the spine and conjure up visions of werewolves and other legendary figures. Conversely, the howling is a way to communicate with or warn others; it is part of their pack mentality and social life which enables them to communicate with each other.

Understanding the amazing creatures that wolves are is the best way to ensure that they roam free for future generations. This beautiful book, with its informative text and stunning photography, celebrates the wonderful qualities that all wolves possess.

ABOVE: The red wolf (Canis lupus rufus) *is native to the southeastern United States. It is a critically endangered species.*

RIGHT: The gray wolf (Canis lupus) *is the most common of the wolf species. It is also known as the timber wolf, western wolf, or simply, wolf. It is native to the wilderness and remote areas of Eurasia and North America.*

THE EVOLUTION & HISTORY OF WOLVES

CHAPTER ONE

THE EVOLUTION & HISTORY
OF WOLVES

The wolf has captured the imagination of people since the beginning of time. Ancient mythologies, written stories, and even cave paintings depict their interactions with humanity. Fossil records further paint the picture of how wolves became a top apex predator and one of the three most populous mammal species in the world at one time, the other two being lions and us!

It may surprise quite a few people to discover that felines and canines are not only related, they come from a common ancestor. This one prehistoric precursor also evolved into bears, raccoons, possums, and other mammals. Although today's specimens do not resemble their original ancestors, genetics do not lie, and this family tree has many varied branches.

PREHISTORIC ANCESTORS OF THE WOLF

The vast majority of biologists believe that wolves developed from an extinct group of primitive mammalian carnivores known as Miacids, which then split into two groups: the Miacidae and the Viverravidae. The Viverravidae consists of feliforms which were cat-like creatures, including cats, hyenas, and mongooses. The Miacidae is where wolves came from, and it includes raccoons, bears, weasels, and dogs as well.

Ancient canids from this time period were often arboreal, meaning they lived in trees, although some resided on the ground also. Like the wolves of today, Miacids had tails and were covered with a layer of fur. Many scientists believe that they were also one of the first mammalian carnivores in the world.

Fossil evidence from the Lower Tertiary period led scientists to believe that Miacids appeared about 52 million years ago. However, the first canid appeared relatively late in the evolutionary history of Miacids. One of these first canids, known as the dawn-wolf, had a

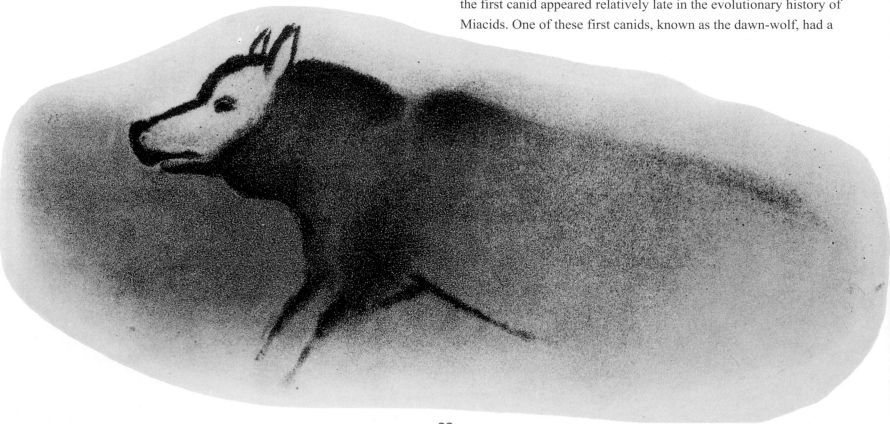

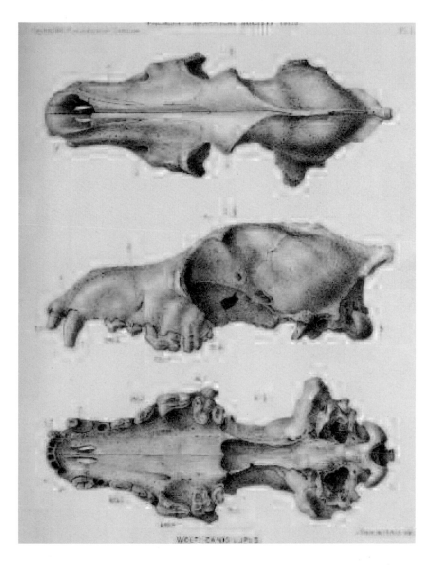

LEFT: Upper Palaeolithic wall painting of a wolf found in a cave at Font-de-Gaume, near Les Eyzies-de-Tayac-Sireuil in the Dordogne, France.

ABOVE: Illustration of a Pleistocene wolf cranium that was found in Kent's Cavern, Torquay, Devon, UK.

OVERLEAF: The gray wolf is one of the world's best-known and most-researched animals, with probably more books written about it than any other wildlife species.

long body and it is likely that it lived in the trees. It is believed to have looked like an elongated fox.

THE PALEOCENE EPOCH

This geological time period lasted from about 66 to 56 million years ago. It was a time of a mass extinction event at the end of the Cretaceous period that marked the demise of giant marine reptiles, non-avian dinosaurs, and most of the other flora and fauna of previous periods.

The North American climate during this period was characterized by a general warming with seasonal variations best described as alternations of wet and dry seasons. One of the most striking features of the vertebrate life during the Paleocene Epoch is the complete lack of dinosaurs and other reptilian groups that dominated the preceding Cretaceous period. Another is the rapid evolution and proliferation of mammals. These Paleocene mammals include representatives of many orders that still are in existence today. However, the forms of these creatures during the Paleocene period were mostly highly specialized.

With the elimination of natural predators like the dinosaurs, an unfilled ecological niche opened worldwide. Large canids, felids, and ursids filled these openings as apex predators. The end of this epoch saw a brief period of extreme climate changes and carbon cycling that further divided these prehistoric ancestors of the wolf. In fact, this period of climate change was the one of the largest and most abrupt events documented in the geological record.

THE MIOCENE EPOCH

The Miocene Epoch saw some of the most diverse ecological changes in history. Many of the mammals that existed underwent drastic evolutionary changes during this period. This was likely due in large part to the vast changes in global climates throughout the era. Warmer temperatures world wide saw the emergence of two new ecosystems: grasslands and kelp forests.

Expanding open vegetations systems like grasslands, tundra, and deserts diminished the availability of closed vegetation such as forests. This overall pattern of biological change led to a rampant diversification of ecosystems and several morphological changes in animals. Mammals such as the Miacids underwent some drastic changes, developing new species to suit the changing environment.

It was during this geological time period that Miacids split into the two groups mentioned earlier, the Miacidae and the Viverravidae. One wolfen ancestor from this period is known as *Tomarctus*. This prehistoric wolf had a fifth toe that evolved over time to become the dew claw evident on canids today. The research of Robert Wayne at the University of California indicates that a number of wolf-like canids diverged from this ancient ancestor.

AELURODON

With a name that means "cat tooth" in Greek, this canid of the North American plains is an immediate descendant of an earlier canid called *Tomarctus*. They were approximately 50 to 75 pounds and 5 feet long. A dog-like build with strong jaws and teeth lent themselves nicely to this canid's carnivorous appetite. There is evidence of a larger species of *Aelurodon* that may have hunted the grassy plains in packs. Research also suggests this larger relative may have been a scavenger.

AMPHICYON

An omnivorous canid, *Amphicyon* means "bear dog" in Greek. In fact, they resembled a small bear with the head of a dog. With a diet more closely related to that of a bear than a wolf, this Miocene canid harkens back to the split of canids, felids, and ursids (bears). The front legs of this prehistoric mammal were particularly well-muscled and may mean that it could stun prey with a single well-aimed swipe of its paw.

The genus *Amphicyon* incorporated nine individual species. The two largest of these weighed up to 400 pounds when fully grown. These massive canids roamed the expanse of the Near East and Europe.

BOROPHAGUS

Another canid of the North American plains was *Borophagus* which means "voracious eater" in Greek. It was one of the larger prehistoric canines. Weighing over 100 pounds and approximately 5 feet long, it was a carnivore and scavenger. In fact, it was the last "hyena dog." These large canids were found in populous groups all over North America. Like its future cousin, *Borophagus* had a wolf-like body with a large head and a strong jaw, strong enough to crush bone. Its extinction two million years ago remains a bit of a mystery.

EPICYON

This large species of prehistoric canid could weigh up to 200 or 300 pounds. With unusually powerful jaws and sharp teeth, its skull was closer in appearance to that of large cat's than a dog's. However, paleontologists have little information about its feeding habits. This megafauna mammal may have hunted in packs or alone. Also, it may have subsisted exclusively on already-dead carcasses, as modern scavengers like coyotes do.

DUSICYON

Exclusive to the Falkland Islands off the coast of Argentina, this was the only mammal on the islands. This means that they did not hunt rats, pigs, or cats but rather birds, insects, and some shellfish. *Dusicyon*, also known as the *Warrah*, is one of the most fascinating and obscure animals to have gone extinct in modern times.

Exactly how *Dusicyon* found its way to the Falklands is somewhat of a mystery. The most likely scenario is that it hitched a ride with early human visitors from South America thousands of years ago. The last *Dusicyon* was killed in 1876. Charles Darwin had briefly studied the *Dusicyon* just prior to this extinction.

EUCYON

With a name that means "original dog" in Greek, the *Eucyon* is actually considered to be the last stage of prehistoric evolution that lead to the appearance of the Canis genus. These prehistoric Miacids were themselves descended from an earlier, smaller ancestor called *Leptocyon*. Extended frontal sinus cavities are believed to relate to the *Eucyon*'s diet and serve to differentiate it from other prehistoric wolf ancestors.

DIRE WOLF

One of the best-known ancestors of today's wolves, many believe this to be a fictitious animal due to its representation in books, movies, and other sources of media. However, it was one of the major apex predators of the Pleistocene Epoch in North America. In fact, it competed for prey with the Saber-Toothed Tiger.

The dire wolf evolved earlier in the North American timeline than the gray wolf and coexisted with it for approximately 400,000 years. A climate change about 16,000 years ago led to the extinction of much of the dire wolf's prey. This, in turn, gradually led to the extinction of the dire wolf itself. That left the gray wolf to dominate and become the prime canine predator in North America.

Although often represented in movies and literature as being unusually large, dire wolves were actually only slightly larger and heavier than the gray wolf. Like many of these prehistoric canids, dire wolves exhibited hyena-like characteristics that included hunting and scavenging food.

LEFT: A 20th century painting of two dire wolves and a saber-toothed tiger surrounding the carcass of a Columbian mammoth at La Rancho Brea tar pits, California, USA.

RIGHT: A skull of a dire wolf.

The main ways in which the dire wolf differs from the gray wolf include:

• Shorter, sturdier legs that may have made it a poor runner.
• A larger, broader head.
• Larger, more massive teeth for crushing bones. Dire wolves are believed to have eaten nearly all of their kill, including bones.
• A smaller braincase that some believe to indicate a lower intelligence than that of the gray wolf.

Much of what is known of the dire wolf is traced to their fossil records. Commonly found in Ice Age sites, these records include several thousand specimens found in the asphalt pits at Rancho La Brea in Los Angeles, California. This is how we know that they

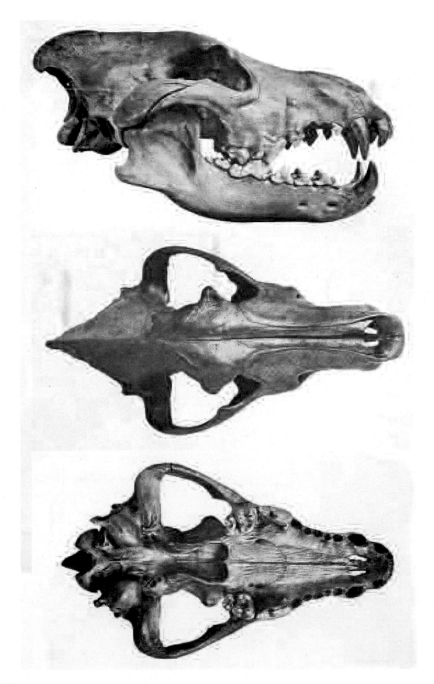

LEFT & OVERLEAF: The gray wolf became a stronger species than the dire wolf, which ultimately led to its extinction.

ABOVE: The coyote is also of the genus canis and like the gray wolf managed to survive extinction.

competed with saber-toothed tigers as their remains are often found together. Clark Kimberling of the University of Evansville is credited with finding the first dire wolf specimen in Evansville, Indiana. It is through this specimen that he then traced the history of the dire wolf.

THE EVOLUTION OF GENUS CANIS

The genus canis includes the gray wolf, coyote, dire wolf, and other prehistoric canids. At the end of the Pleistocene Epoch, these canids underwent very different fates. While coyotes and gray wolves survived the extinction event, others such as the dire wolf did not. Paleontologists believe that each of these species comes from a different evolutionary lineage within the genus. Meaning that none of them are the direct ancestor of the others.

THE HISTORY OF WOLVES

Long before Native Americans and the Inuit people crossed the Beringia (also known as the Bering Land Bridge) into North America, the gray wolf was well established. The relationship that developed between these indigenous peoples and the wolves is evidenced in their art and stories. These most often depicted the wolf and man joined as one powerful creature. In fact, some legends have the wolf healing warriors, saving people from the great flood, and protecting the tribe. Some legends show the wolf as a trickster as well.

There was a time when wolves roamed nearly all of North America. Roughly half a million wolves lived in harmony with nature and side by side with Native Americans. The kind of brotherhood that Native Americans had with the wolves they shared the land with was not seen in other areas of the world.

NATIVE AMERICANS

One of the most well known Native American legends comes from the Cherokee. Known as Two Wolves, this legend cements the bond between man and animal by showing how similar the two truly are. In the legend, an old Cherokee chief is teaching his grandson about life as a man.

"There is a terrible war inside me," the grandfather says. "It is a terrible fight between two wolves. One of these wolves is pure evil filled with ego, false pride, inferiority, guilt, arrogance, regret, envy, anger, sorrow, greed, self-pity, resentment, lies, and superiority. The other wolf is good. He is faith, truth, empathy, kindness, serenity, love, joy, peace, hope, humility, benevolence, generosity, and compassion."

The grandfather then looked at his grandson and said, "The same war is going on inside of you and every other person too."

After thinking about these statements for some time, the grandson asked his grandfather which wolf would win the battle. To which the old Cherokee replied, "The one you feed."

While this tale may seem philosophical in nature, it is also symbolic of the relationship between wolves and man. With the wolf

embodying both the ultimate negativity as well as the overwhelming positivity, it represents the struggle within each person. Like people, the wolf is neither good nor evil but rather somewhere in the middle.

EUROPE

Conversely, wolves throughout the "old country" were seen as evil incarnate and the slaughter began. Wolves once graced nearly all of Europe with their presence. However, conflicts with humans and fears originating from myths, folklore, and religious beliefs drove on a persecution. Their main prey throughout this area consisted largely of ungulate species—those with hooves. This included livestock such as horses, sheep, goats, cattle, etc.

LEFT & OVERLEAF: Fine examples of Eurasian wolves in the forests of Sumava, Czech Republic.

ABOVE: A male Italian wolf in the mountainous Piedmont area of northern Italy.

Today, several subspecies of wolf can be found in the Eurasian area. Examples include:

- **Tundra wolf** (*Canis lupus albus*). Also known as the Eurasian Arctic wolf, it is one of the largest subspecies of gray wolf. This specimen can still be found in the northern reaches of Canada and Russia and into the Arctic.

- **Russian wolf** (*Canis lupus communis*). There is evidence to suggest that the Russian wolf is thriving again in Russia. A "super pack" of over 400 individuals has been observed.

- **Italian Wolf** (*Canis lupus italicus*). Also known as the Apennine Wolf, it was native to the Apennine mountains and the Alps. It has seen a recent resurgence.

- **Eurasian Wolf** (*Canis lupus lupus*). Also known as the common wolf, steppes wolf, Tibetan wolf, and Chinese wolf.

- **Indian Wolf** (Canis lupus pallipes). Also known as the Desert Wolf.

- **Iberian Wolf** (*Canis lupus signatus*). It still inhabits the forest and plains of northern Portugal and northwestern Spain.

33

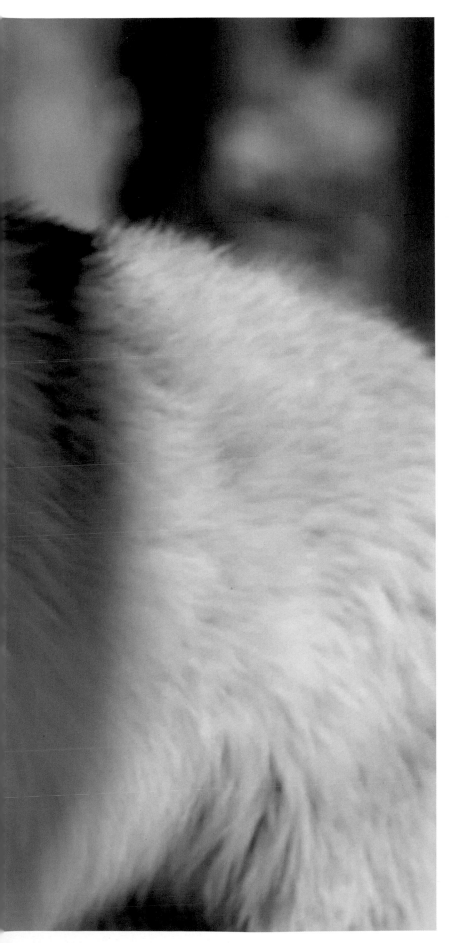

In England, hunting with horses and dogs along with trapping in cages, traps, and pits completely obliterated their existence by the early 1500s. Scotland killed its last wolf in the mid-1700s and most other European countries followed suit not long after. Somehow a few wolves managed to survive in the Middle East, Spain, Italy, Germany, India, and eastern Europe. However, it is unknown how many wolves survive today in China and Russia.

This animosity toward wolves in Eurasia grew from myths, fables, and legends from the Middle Ages. Many legends from this period connected wolves with the dark powers of the supernatural world. They were believed to be in league with evil forces and even Satan himself. This compelled people to feel justified and even righteous in their extermination of the wolf.

LEFT: The tundra wolf is a subspecies of gray wolf native to Eurasia's tundra and forest-tundra zones from Finland to the Kamchatka Peninsula in far eastern Russia.

ABOVE: The Indian wolf is a subspecies of gray wolf that ranges from southwest Asia to the Indian subcontinent.

COLONIAL AMERICA

In the New World, there were two top predators—men and wolves. Unable to avoid one another, these two species clashed over space and livestock. When colonists first came to North America, they brought their traditional European hatred of the wolf with them. They attacked wolves with traps, pits, and even poison. Bounties were paid for hides and body parts throughout the colonial and revolutionary time. However, the American war on wolves did not really get underway until the 1800s.

During this period, more people began to move into the Great Plains area that wolves had traditionally a free reign in. In fact,

LEFT: The Iberian wolf is quite different from the Eurasian wolf. It has a slighter frame, white marks on the upper lips, dark marks on the tail, and a pair of dark marks in its front legs.

ABOVE & OVERLEAF: Wolf numbers in colonial America suffered greatly. Hunters or "wolfers" attempted to eradicate them altogether.

Native Americans coexisted with enormous herds of buffalo and wolves, living in peace. When the settlers arrived, they commenced the systematic destruction of the wolf in a number of ways.

In addition to the trapping, hunting, and poisoning of these amazing creatures, settlers took aim at the wolf's primary food sources. Massive overhunting of buffalo and deer left little for the wolves to eat, which drove them into the settlements. This, in turn, was seen as a threat and increased the settlers' animosity towards the wild wolf. Furthermore, European markets paid well for the thick winter wolf fur that could be made into garments.

As sheep and cattle grazing expanded, increasingly more wolf packs were wiped out to protect the livestock of settlers. The most common way that American wolfers (wolf hunters) eradicated wolves was by using Strychnine placed on the carcasses of dead sheep, cattle, and buffalo. Strychnine poisoning is a painful and slow death, and the risk of contamination of other animals was ever present.

There are no definite numbers of how many wolves were killed during the last half of the nineteenth century. However, the anti-wolf

campaign during this period was most active in the western part of the United States where the majority of wolves still lived and hunted. Still, it is estimated that somewhere between one and two million wolves were slaughtered, if not more.

AFRICA

Although it was long believed that there were no wolves on the continent of Africa but rather only jackals, recent discoveries have proven otherwise. The African Wolf (*Canis anthus*), once considered a subspecies of the golden jackal, has been proven through genetic testing to actually be a subspecies of gray wolf that had otherwise not been seen.

The African wolf is darker and larger than the golden jackal. Furthermore, it behaves differently. African wolves are often more shy and solitary than golden jackals. The only interaction observed between these two now distinct species was when wolves would fight for the carcasses the golden jackals were eating. The jackals always backed down to the wolves in the end.

LEFT: *The African wolf is a canid native to north and northeastern Africa. The species commonly occurs from Senegal in the west to Egypt in the east, in a range including Morocco, Algeria, Tunisia, and Libya in the north to Nigeria, Chad, and Tanzania in the south.*

ABOVE: *A dingo* (Canis lupus dingo) *on the beach in Great Sandy National Park, Fraser Island Waddy Point, Queensland, Australia. The dingo is Australia's answer to the wolf.*

AUSTRALIA

No naturally occurring species of Canis Lupus exists on the continent of Australia. However, the Australian Dingo (*Canis lupus dingo*) was brought to the country over four thousand years ago by settlers from southeast Asia.

Since that time, this small vulpine wolf has become a regular fixture of the Australian Outback. Today, the dingo is classified as a vulnerable group, as reported by the International Union for Conservation of Nature Red List of Threatened Species. However, they are not considered to be endangered.

SOUTH AMERICA

The canids of South America are mostly related to the fox. Those canids that are Canis Lupus are referred to as "zorros" in this area. These zorros are found in every habitat in South America from the coastal deserts to the open savanna. Even the rain forests boast a zorro called the Small-Eared Zorro (*Dusicyon microtis*). It is unusual since canids in other areas avoid these environments. South America even has a crab-eating zorro (*Cerdocyon thous*) that inhabits lowland forests and coastal regions.

The most unusual canid in South America is the maned wolf (*Chrysocyon brachyurus*). Although not exactly a wolf, this canid is the largest in South America and the only member of the genus Chrysocyon. With a thick red coat, erect ears, and long black legs, the maned wolf evolved to dominate in tall grass savannas. It stands approximately 3 feet tall at the shoulder and weighs in at roughly 50 pounds.

Ranging throughout central and eastern South America, the maned wolf inhabits the cerrado. This is the largest biome of South America and is made up of grasslands, marshes, wet and dry forests, wetlands, and savannas. Both Brazil and Argentina are carefully monitoring the maned wolf population and have established captive breeding programs to help ensure the existence of the maned wolf for future generations.

LEFT: The small-eared zorro (Dusicyon microtis) *can be found in the Amazon rainforest region of South America (in Peru, Bolivia, Brazil, Colombia, Ecuador, and possibly Venezuela).*

*BELOW: The maned wolf (*Chrysocyon brachyurus*) is the largest canid of South America. Its markings resemble those of foxes, but it is not a fox, nor is it a wolf. It is the only species in the genus Chrysocyon.*

THE TWENTIETH CENTURY

With the aggressive attack on wolves in full swing, it is not surprising that by 1900 there were few wolves left in the western United States. Those that still existed continued to be hunted with the full support of the government. Even President Theodore Roosevelt, widely known for his environmental activism, declared the wolf to be a "beast of waste and destruction" and called for its continued eradication.

In 1919, the United States government passed a law that called for the extermination of wolves on federally owned lands. Before its repeal in 1942, the government estimated another 25,000 wolves were killed. Unfortunately for the wolf, however, the campaign did not end there.

1960s PERSECUTION & EXTERMINATION

Humanity continued to wage war against the wolf and by the 1960s, the wolf had almost been exterminated completely. The United States government implemented yet another policy for wolf control based on the view that wolves were pests that posed a threat to the continued

ABOVE, RIGHT & OVERLEAF: Wolves in the United States had a tough period from colonial times until the 1970s when it was finally realized that they needed conservation and protection.

prosperity and safety of the American people. Skulls and skins were piled high to claim bounties as well as for trophy photographs. People from this period considered it a service to God and country by ridding it of such "vermin."

By the year 1960, the gray wolf was fundamentally extinct throughout the majority of its traditional range. The deep woods of upper Michigan and Minnesota were home to the last 300 wild wolves in the lower 48 states. These packs only survived by running and hiding at the first sign of humans.

Officially, the war on wolves ended for the majority of the United States in the late 1960s. Unofficially though, many hunters tried in vain to find the last of the northern timber wolves (another name for the gray wolf). Luckily, these wolves held their ground and began to make a slight comeback throughout the end of the 1960s.

1970s A SLOW NATURAL RECOVERY

By 1970 there were a few reports of wolf sightings farther south than had been seen in over a decade. When the Great Lakes area holdouts were joined by a Canadian immigration of wolves, their numbers began to slowly climb. As public interest and concern began to form over the possibility of extinction, the Endangered Species List was created. In 1973, the Endangered Species Act was passed; it invoked severe fines and possible jail time for killing the nearly extinct gray wolf, or indeed any other wolf in the United States.

The south of the United States was home to the Mexican wolf (*Canis lupus baileyi*). These wolves were smaller than their northern

BELOW & RIGHT: Both the gray wolf (below & overleaf) and the red wolf (right) were hunted to near extinction.

cousins and had sandy-colored fur much like the sands of the deserts in which they often lived. They lived in smaller packs, likely due in part to smaller, less nutritious food sources in their desert homes. Unfortunately, the Endangered Species Act came too late for the Mexican wolf as it had completely disappeared from the American southwest by 1970.

1980s THE BEGINNING OF CONSERVATION

After the creation of the Endangered Species Act, public fascination with wolves grew rapidly. It seemed that people just could not get enough about wolves. This opened new avenues of growth for the wolf populations across the United States and into Canada and Mexico as well. However, the wild Mexican wolf still went extinct in Mexico by 1980. Furthermore, by this time the smaller red wolf survived only in captivity as it went extinct in the wild decades prior.

In an effort to preserve the Mexican wolf, the Endangered Species Act pushed for the capture of the last female and last four males. It was hoped that through a captive breeding program the Mexican wolf could someday be reintroduced into the wild.

During this same period, a pack of northern gray wolves crossed the Canadian border into Glacier National Park in Montana. To celebrate the renewed wolf population in that once barren area, the pack was dubbed the *Magic Pack*. Today, there are around 500 wolves living in the park. Their numbers have to be carefully managed and monitored to ensure their survival for the future.

1990s RED WOLVES RISING

The red wolf (*Canis lupus rufus*) is an entirely distinct species from the gray wolf. Smaller in size with a reddish coloration that gives it its name, they are often described as appearing to be a hybrid of a coyote and a gray wolf. It is believed that these canids lived all along the east coast and southeast portions of the United States at one time.

As with most other wolves, these crimson canines were hunted to extinction throughout their natural range. However, by 1990 the first red wolves were reintroduced into the wild in North Carolina.

BELOW & RIGHT: The red wolf was extinct in the wild, but in the late 1980s some were reintroduced into North Carolina.

Meanwhile, the gray wolf population of the Great Lakes region continued to thrive and grow. Spreading deeper into northern Wisconsin, these packs merged with more that had migrated down from Canada, a trend that was becoming increasingly common. With Montana's Magic Pack producing the first wild packs in decades, population growth continued.

It was in the early 1990s that the first substantial reports of wolf sightings were made in the Cascade Mountains of Washington State. This era also saw the most states in decades boasting wolf populations.

BELOW, RIGHT & OVERLEAF: A combination of packs gradually migrating down from Canada and reintroductions into some American states saw wolf numbers begin to rise in the 1990s.

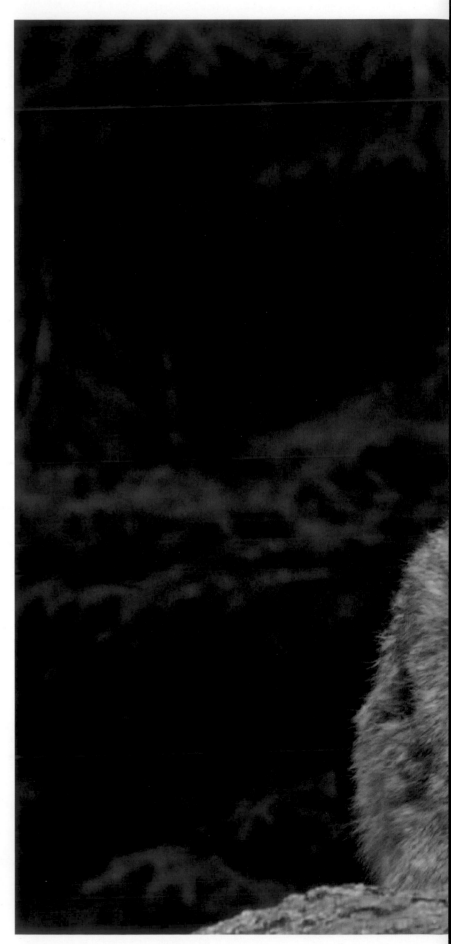

1995 & 1996 THE NORTHERN ROCKIES REINTRODUCTION

After years of political battles and grassroots efforts to win over local ranchers, Yellowstone National Park and the state of Idaho undertook a reintroduction effort for the gray wolf. The plan called for 31 Canadian gray wolves to be released into Yellowstone and another 23 into the Frank Church Wilderness of Idaho.

The effort began in Idaho with the "hard release" of wolves. A hard release means that the wolves are trapped in their natural range and released into the new area directly from the crates with no acclimatization process. This process was less effective than officials had hoped for as the wolves were drawn to return to their home. In fact, one female traveled over 60 miles in one day in an effort to locate her Canadian home.

It was at this point that the Nez Perce Nation took over the reintroduction effort in Idaho. This time around, the wolves were kept in backcountry pens for three months to acclimatize them to their new home. The reintroduction worked well the second time around and the process was repeated with the Yellowstone reintroductions.

ABOVE: Protected and free. A pack running through Yellowstone National Park. Canadian gray wolves were released into the park in the 1990s.

EXTINCT WOLVES

Despite the best efforts of mankind to fix its ecological mistake, some wolf populations are gone forever. These include:

- **Kenai Peninsula Wolf** (*Canis lupus alces*). An extinct subspecies of gray wolf that only lived on the remote Kenai Peninsula in Alaska.
- **Newfoundland Wolf** (*Canis lupus brothucus*) also known as the Labrador Wolf. This extinct subspecies of gray wolf was native to Newfoundland.
- **Bernard's Wolf** (*Canis lupus bernardi*). Native to Banks Island and Victoria Island in the Northwest Territories of Canada, this subspecies of the gray wolf was hunted to extinction.
- **Manitoba Wolf** (*Canis lupus griseoalbus*). Whether or not this wolf existed is debated among scientists. If it did exist, it does not anymore.
- **Honshu Wolf** (*Canis lupus hodophilax*). This wolf was native to Japan and was the smallest subspecies of gray wolf. It was once revered in Japanese culture, but rabies and hunting led to its extinction with the last one being killed in 1905.
- **Hokkaido Wolf** (*Canis lupus hattai*). Another Japanese wolf that no longer exists, this subspecies of the gray wolf was a fairly large animal. It was wiped out during the Meiji restoration, a political revolution. As often happens with wolves, the government at the time decided that this wolf was a threat to ranching and paid bounties for pelts.
- **Texas Wolf** (*Canis lupus monstrabilis*). Considered a close relative of the Mexican wolf, this subspecies was last seen in the 1940s.
- **Florida Black Wolf** (*Canis lupus floridanus*). Extinct in the early 1900s due largely to human population expansion into their natural habitats. This wolf is similar to the red wolf in every way other than the color of its fur.

The extinction of these major players in the food chain has more far reaching effects than simply never seeing that animal again in the wild. When the number of carnivorous predators diminish, the population of their prey species can increase, causing an upset in the predator-prey relationship. Throughout the world, in areas where top predator numbers have been reduced, the number of prey animals has often risen sharply to the detriment of their own species and the environment. Disease in deer in North America is now more common than when wolves were prevalent. This is a perfect example of a consequence of removing one top predator from the natural world.

THE TWENTY-FIRST CENTURY

Thanks to the repopulation and conservation efforts, the North American gray wolf population was estimated to be 78,000 individuals at the beginning of this century. North American countries have enacted laws to protect wolves and this is helping to raise the numbers. Some Eurasian wolves have also seen a resurgence in recent years by naturally recolonizing some areas.

In the United States, at least 13 states now have wolf populations. The reintroduction of this important species is an essential part of rebalancing the natural environment. The most well-documented of these programs was the reintroduction of wolves into the Yellowstone National Park. There were several positive knock-on effects of this reintroduction, but a key one was when the wolf-fearing elk moved away from rivers. This in turn, led to the recovery of riverine vegetation, which then increased the populations of songbirds, beavers, and other important species.

ABOVE: A white wolf or Arctic wolf (Canis lupus arctos) lives in the Arctic regions of North America and Greenland.

RIGHT: The black wolf is genetically a gray wolf (Canis lupus).

OVERLEAF: Thanks to government legislation and conservation efforts, gray wolf numbers are on the increase.

THE WORLD OF
THE WOLF

CHAPTER TWO

THE WORLD OF
OF THE WOLF

When we think about where wolves live, we imagine a distant, far off wilderness full of danger and adventure. However, while wolves are clearly found in pockets throughout the world, their favored territories are swamps, coastal prairies, and forests. We tend to imagine that wolves only live in colder climates, but wolves can live in temperatures that range from minus 70 to 120 degrees Fahrenheit. They are also prolific nomads, for they don't like to stay in one place. They are known travel as far as 12 miles per day as part of their daily routine.

Wolves are highly social animals that live in familial type groups called packs. These packs have a highly complex social structure and often contain somewhere between five and ten individuals. However, recently some packs have been seen with more than 30 members. Within the pack, all members work together for the benefit of the community as a whole. Raising pups, hunting for food, protecting the pack, and territory, are shared responsibilities that every individual takes part in.

BELOW LEFT: This wolf's expression is showing aggression. Wolves are very sophisticated in the way they communicate with other pack members.

BELOW: Just like our domestic dog, the wolf employs a variety of facial expressions. The wolf uses this body language to communicate with other pack members.

ABOVE & OVERLEAF: Wolves live for around six years. However, there are reports of some individuals living thirteen years.

While there are many subspecies of wolf, all with an array of different traits and characteristics, most of us tend to know the gray wolf best. These beautiful misunderstood animals are the most common type of wolf and therefore, the most photographed and

written about. Even though our understanding of the wolf over the last 30 years has improved enormously, many of us still consider the wolf an animal to fear. This perpetuates the misconception that wolves are dangerous to man.

This image of a wolf with its hackles raised is a common one. However, our interpretation of this facial expression as a sign of aggression is based solely on lack of knowledge. When a wolf, or even a domestic dog for that matter, raises its hackles, it may be for a number of reasons including being startled, excited, aroused, or threatened; it could even be a sign of interest in something.

This physical reaction is similar to that which human's experience when the hair goes up on their arms, or more accurately, the back of one's neck. As with people, a number of stimuli can cause this involuntary physical reaction.

The gray wolf is a substantial animal and therefore, it is understandable why an animal of this size could be considered intimidating and fearsome. Gray wolves range from three to six feet in length, and that is just their head and body. Their tails make them appear even larger and can be up to two feet long by themselves. With average weights of up to 175 pounds and heights reaching three feet at the shoulder, these are large formidable apex predators to be sure. A vigorous respect of any animal such as the gray wolf is wise, but fear is unnecessary.

According to *National Geographic*, the gray wolf can live for an average of six to eight years in the wild. However, there is evidence that some individuals, tracked in the United States, were known to have lived up to thirteen years. In captivity, life expectancy is better, with some wolves living up to 16 years of age.

In the wild, wolves die primarily from starvation and territorial fights with other wolves. Diseases such as canine parvovirus and mange can also cause death. In fact, these two diseases are currently a treat to recovering wolf populations around the world. The most significant threat to the wolf, however, is through human activity including the destruction of the wolf's prey and habitat, illegal (and in some places, legal) hunting, automobile accidents, etc.

Within their territories, the gray wolf is one of the chief carnivorous hunters of large hoofed animals such as buffalo, elk,

ABOVE & RIGHT: Eurasian wolves hunting for prey in eastern Europe.

moose, musk oxen, caribou, and deer. Their ideal target are the young, old, sick, or injured members of these animals' groupings. However, the gray wolf's diet depends strongly on which prey animals are available at any one time. Wolves also hunt and eat smaller mammals like beavers, birds, rabbits, mountain goats, etc. Of course, if there are livestock animals within the range of a gray wolf, it will happily eat those too.

The wolf is a keystone species, which means it is a species that other species depend upon within a biome. If that keystone species is removed for any reason, the entire ecosystem could be irrevocably changed. In a natural environment and without the influence of man, the wolf is at the top of the food chain. This means it has no natural predators. When top predator numbers fall, prey populations grow in an unrestricted manner, leading to overpopulation of the prey species, upsetting the whole balance of nature.

LIFE IN THE PACK

Wolves are not solitary creatures. The image of a lone wolf is popular, but far from accurate. If a wolf is spotted in the wild alone it is because it is scouting for its pack or looking to start its own. Moreover, it is unlikely that a wolf will be alone for long. A lone wolf may attempt to join another family of wolves, and will occasionally be accepted by them.

Most packs represent a family unit with a dominant male and dominant female, known as alphas. They are the authoritarians of the pack much like the mother and father of a family. The rest of the pack is generally made up of the offspring of those alphas. The social hierarchy is also divided along gender lines. That is, the alpha male rules over all the male wolves and the alpha female leads the female wolves.

"I woke up one morning thinking about wolves and realized that wolf packs function as families. Everyone has a role, and if you act within the parameters of your role, the whole pack succeeds, and when that falls apart, so does the pack."
~ Jodi Picoult, American author.

LEFT & OVERLEAF: The Arctic wolf (Canis lupus arctos)*, also known as the white wolf or polar wolf, is a subspecies of gray wolf native to northern North America and Greenland. It is relatively small wolf with a striking white or light gray coat.*

The alphas of a pack establish the pack's territorial boundaries, choose den sites, and lead the hunt for food. Moreover, the alphas are the first to eat, with the male getting the first meal and the female following. The other wolves in the pack will not begin eating until the alpha pair have eaten their fill. Even after that, the hierarchy within the pack dictates who eats and who waits to eat down the line.

The size of a pack is related to the size of its territory. Both are governed by the amount of available prey. In good times when pack numbers start to rise, a second pair of wolves will step up as the beta

ABOVE: The alpha male will be the first to eat and will control the pack's comings and goings. The alphas retain their control over the pack by constantly asserting themselves in a dominant way.

RIGHT: A gray wolf showing submissive behavior to an alpha male.

OVERLEAF: Wolves are very sociable animals and are constantly interacting with each other to affirm their place in the pack.

pair. The beta male is the second in command to the alpha male. He is the wolf that steps up to lead if something happens to the current alpha. The duties of the beta pair mirror those of the alphas.

There is also a recognizable position at the bottom of the wolf social hierarchy. The lowest member is known as the omega. These wolves are often the target of scorn and aggression from other members of the pack.

There is always something to do within the wolf pack. There are pups that need tending and educating, young adults that must be controlled as they become more assertive, old wolves that must be cared for, territorial boundaries to establish and enforce, hunting to be

ABOVE: The alpha male and female are the only members of the pack that are allowed to mate. In some situations, however, betas will be permitted to mate.

RIGHT: Eurasian juvenile wolves playing in the snow in Belarus.

OVERLEAF: Alpha male and female Arctic wolves.

done, and so much more. The entire pack is responsible for sharing these duties, even the alphas and betas. There are no lazy leaders in a wolf pack.

In addition to leading the pack, the alphas are the only members of the pack that are allowed to mate.

FAMILY LIFE

Generally speaking, the alphas are the only wolves within a pack that breed and consequently, the alpha male will only mate with the alpha female. While the majority of research shows that these two animals do, in fact, become pair-bonded that does not mean that they are

bound together for life. Pair-bonding is a term used by biologist to describe the establishment of a close rapport with one other animal by way of courtship and sexual activity. Essentially, pair-bonding is a more academic term for a marriage— albeit a common law marriage.

This loyalty and monogamy is essential to the successful continuation of the pack. If all the members of a pack were allowed to mate, it would create conditions that would likely destroy the pack. For one, the rapid increase in the number of mouths to feed would place undue stress on the prey populations. Secondly, rampant inbreeding leads to genetic weakness and disease that creates ever increasingly weaker animals. Finally, if each female pack member had

a litter of her own pups to take care of, there would be no way to share responsibilities, essential to the survival of the pack.

By bonding to his mate, the alpha male becomes an attentive father to the pups that he sires. This builds a bond between father and offspring, which then becomes loyalty and respect as the young grow into adulthood.

MATING
Female wolves are able to breed at two years of age. However, most do not breed until they are three years or more due to the pack social structure. If a female wolf does not become the alpha or beta of a pack by five years of age, she will likely never breed.

ABOVE: A Eurasian wolf and her pups. Usually, it is only the alpha male and the alpha female that can breed.

RIGHT: Pups are not just looked after by their mother and father, other wolves will step in to help raise them.

LEFT & OVERLEAF: An alpha female gray wolf. Depending on conditions, wolves mate in early spring and give birth 63 days later.

ABOVE: The den is created by all pack members for the alpha female to raise her young in.

Late winter or early spring is the prime period to mate for most wolves. Depending upon the specific type of wolf, where it resides, and other outside factors, this may vary slightly. However, for the most part, following mating, wolves give birth in late spring or early summer in most of North America.

THE DEN

After mating, wolves create birthing dens to house the mother and pups after they are born. The alpha male will generally scout out a safe place for the den and then the female alpha, with the assistance of her subordinates, will dig out the den. These small hidden dens are often made in hollowed out logs, well-drained meadows near water, under tree roots, in rocky outcroppings, or sometimes even in abandoned beaver lodges.

These dens may be used for several years, but sometimes, an alpha female may decide to move her den with every litter.

PUPS

With a gestation period of 63 days, most litters are born between March and June—spring in North America. Generally, wolves have only one litter per season. These litters average five to six pups which are born both blind and deaf and weigh under a pound each. Newborn wolf pups all have blue eyes that slowly change to either yellow, green, or brown over the first eight months of their life.

Once the pups arrive, the mother wolf stays in the birthing den with them for the first three weeks of their lives. They need to nurse every four to six hours. During this time, the mother is brought food by the entire pack and attended to by her subordinated females as well as by the alpha male. Studies show, that the time the alpha male and the alpha female spend together while the pups are young, strengthens their mutual bond and also strengthens their domination over the rest of the pack.

After that initial three-week period, the alpha female can come and go from the birthing den while the pups stay in the den until they are older. The mother continues to nurse the pups but the entire pack helps guard and care for them.

Once the pups reach the age of eight weeks, they are weaned. Still not quite ready for solid food, the pups begin eating semi-solid food that has been prechewed by the alpha female. This continues for

BELOW, RIGHT & OVERLEAF: Wolf pups are born with blue eyes. However, over some months they change to yellow, brown, or green.

roughly another two months until the pups are around four months old and can eat solid food.

At this time, the birthing den is abandoned entirely until the next litter comes. The pups are moved to a carefully chosen open area that researchers have dubbed the "rendezvous site." Here the pups will spend the rest of the summer learning how to live and behave within the pack. When the rest of the pack hunts, the pubs are guarded by a few adult members of the pack in this rendezvous site.

ABOVE: When they are very young the pups will stay close to their mother or another adult.

RIGHT & OVERLEAF: As the pups mature they become more independent. By eight weeks they are weaned.

ACQUIESCENCE OR DISPERSAL

By the end of the summer, the pups will be around six to eight months of age and are ready to become proper members of the pack. If they choose to stay with the pack they are born to, they will start joining in hunts and traveling with the pack. If they decide to leave the pack, they must venture out on their own to find and join or create a new pack.

The young wolves who choose to leave will travel to other available territories in the area, although some travel quite far, with the average being 65 miles. However, tracking through satellite collar has shown that some offspring can travel more than 1,000 miles from their birthplace in under 4 months.

Wolves will not stay solitary for long, if they fail to create or join their own pack, they will often return to their familial pack. These

BELOW: The coat color of the gray wolf can vary from black, red, gray, and cream. This is due to genetic variation.

RIGHT: A juvenile gray wolf will either stay with the pack of its birth or leave to find a new pack.

"disgraced" wolves usually end up at the bottom of the pack's hierarchy. These omega wolves will never be allowed to mate and will often be the target of aggression. They are also the very last to eat.

HUNTING & DIET

Contrary to widely held belief, wolves do not eat people. In fact, there has never been a recorded instance of a wolf eating a person—ever. Moreover, there has never been a report of a healthy wolf even attacking a person. In the vernacular of the current climate, wolves attacking and eating people is fake news.

BELOW & RIGHT: The omega wolf is the lowest of the pack. They are often the subject of aggression from other wolves in the pack and are always last to eat.

OVERLEAF: A large pack of Canadian gray wolves. Pack sizes depend on the availability of food.

A WOLF'S DIET

The common prey gray wolves hunt is mostly large, hoofed animals including different kinds of deer, mountain goats, moose, elk, and bison. They will also hunt hares, beavers, birds, and fish.

Coastal wolves will also eat migrating salmon, crabs, mussels, and other oceanic creatures that reside in their territory. If all else fails, wolves will even eat berries, insects, and lizards. Essentially, wolves will eat whatever is available.

THE EATING ROUTINE OF THE WOLF

Have you heard the saying "wolfing it down?" While they can go more than a week without eating, when they do eat they can eat up to 20 pounds of meat in one meal. That is a lot of meat. Accordingly,

ABOVE: An Arctic wolf eating part of a deer that was caught by the pack. The alphas and betas eat first followed by the rest of the pack.

RIGHT: A pack of Eurasian wolves on the scent of their prey.

LEFT & ABOVE: While wolves prefer a diet of hoofed animals, they will hunt and kill smaller animals too.

wolves who do eat that much in one sitting go inactive for a day or two. With that much food to digest, it is hard for the wolf to do much else. When considering that wolf hunts are successful only eight percent of the time on average, it is not surprising that they gorge themselves when they can, to make it through if they do not eat again for more than a week.

On average, the wolf eats between 5 and 14 pounds of meat a day. However, this obviously does not mean that they eat every day. Wolves survive largely by hunting, however they are opportunistic by nature, so they will also scavenge or even raid garbage if they live close to human habitation.

HOW WOLVES HUNT

The strict pack structure that wolves live in is not simply for social interaction. The pack is essential for bringing down the large prey that is the wolf's main diet. The wolf is an instinctive hunter and its pack is a finely tuned unit.

Wolves have roughly 200 million scent receptors in their noses. Human beings have only five million. They use this highly sensitive sense of smell to locate wounded, sick, or old animals for which to hunt. They can smell their prey from more than a mile away. Their other senses are also highly tuned to the business of hunting. For

example, wolves can hear for nearly six miles within a forest and more than ten miles on the open prairie or tundra.

While wolves cannot run as fast as some of the animals they hunt, their incredible stamina gives them the ability to chase their prey for prolonged periods of time. By wearing their prey down, they can then surround the animal and take it down together. However, wolves will as a rule, not attack an animal that is standing still. They will wait hours or even days for the animal to run before attacking it.

Wolves are patient, determined hunters. In western North America, researchers have observed that wolves track their prey up and down the mountainside. The wolves in the study, clearly had an understanding of their prey's behaviour. Grazing animals are known to

LEFT & ABOVE: Wolves have incredible senses of smell and hearing. This enables them to locate their prey from a great distance away.

go to higher elevations in the summer and return to lower elevations for the winter months and this was something the wolves know about. While wolves will rarely follow migrating prey outside of their territories, they will follow them to different elevations within their ranges.

TERRITORY & RANGE

Wolves live in wide range habitats that include grasslands, forests, mountains, coastal areas, plains, and deserts. This means that there are few areas of the world that are not hospitable to wolves. However, the primary requirement for a wolf pack is to have a large, remote territory that is free from human disturbance. Unfortunately, that is something that is hard to find today.

At one time, in the not so distant past, wolves covered nearly every part of the world. In North America, the gray wolf claimed the territory from the Atlantic to the Pacific and from mid-Mexico to the southern fringe of Greenland. Those historic ranges disappeared over

ABOVE: The Iberian wolf has a limited range. This is because its natural habitat has been encroached upon by humans. Today, the Iberian inhabits only the wildest regions of northwest Spain and Portugal.

RIGHT: The Arctic wolf, however, has a much larger range of wilderness to live in, so its numbers are healthy and it is not endangered.

time. Today, wolves occupy just of small percentage of the former area that they once did within North America.

Populations of wolves in the lower 48 of the United States are currently found in Washington's Cascade mountains, northwestern Montana, the Upper peninsula of Michigan, central Idaho, northeastern Minnesota, northern Wisconsin, West Virginia, California, Oregon, Arizona, New Mexico, North Carolina, and

BELOW, RIGHT & OVERLEAF: The gray wolf used to inhabit vast swathes of North America. However, after being virtually wiped out in the 1900s, together with a dramatic increase in human populations, the wolf's range has been considerably reduced.

Wyoming. The vast majority of these populations are due to conservation efforts including reintroduction. Conversely, the wolf populations of Alaska and Canada still cover more than two thirds of their historic range.

Wolves are known to traverse long distances within their range. Often, they cover many miles per day. Thus, their territories need to be rather expansive. In Minnesota, researchers estimate pack territories to range from 55 to 120 square miles. Moreover, in the western part of the United States, researchers gauge wolf pack territories at a whopping 75 to 150 square miles. An interesting trend is the reduction of a territory size in winter months as prey animals are clustered on their wintering fields.

COMMUNICATION & HOWLING

While the wolf's howl has long been associated with the night and the moon, there is nothing sinister in this. The reason why wolves howl at night is because they are primarily nocturnal, and they point their heads towards the moon and stars for acoustic reasons. This allows their howls to travel as far as possible. Howling is the way in which wolves socialize with each other. Wolves howl to locate other members of their pack, to warn off intruders, and mostly to communicate. If a lone wolf howls, it is likely that it is trying to attract the attention of its pack.

Communal howling, where the entire pack howl together, serves a number of functions. It can be used to for territorial communications between one pack and another. Moreover, the alpha may start a communal howl as a demonstration of its power within the pack. These group howling sessions might also simply be the result of one or two individual members of the pack getting stirred up and spurring those around them on.

LEFT: The Eurasian wolf inhabits some of the more remote forests of eastern Europe. These wolves have been photographed in Romania.

Howling is not the only way that wolves communicate. They also use a lot of body language to get their meaning across to other members of the pack and outsiders alike.

A submissive wolf will tuck its tail between its legs, pin its ears back, and roll onto its back to expose its stomach. It will also expose its throat. A wolf lower down in the pack will use these submissive postures more often than the more dominant wolves nearer the top of the hierarchy. Omega wolves use this body language regularly to avoid confrontation with other wolves in the pack. However, this common posture is at times adopted by all members of the pack to relay to others, quite simply, that they do not want to fight.

When a wolf approaches an alpha of its pack, it assumes a similarly submissive posture. However, in this instance the wolf will not roll on its back. Instead, it will approach the alpha, holding its body low to the ground, almost like a crawl. Its ears will be flattened against its head and its tail will be held between its legs.

BELOW & OVERLEAF: Howling is an important aspect of pack behavoir. It enables wolves to communicate with each other.

RIGHT: Two young gray wolves display submissive behavior to a more dominant male.

120

The alpha, however, will adopt a competely different posture. It will approach a fellow pack member with its head and tail held high and its ears perked up. This communicates confidence and strength to the other wolf. Subordinate wolves will also use this type of body language to communicate their lack of fear to a challenger.

When a wolf is feeling playful, it will try to encourage others to play with it by charging around enthusiastically. Just like a domestic dog, a wolf will bow its head while raising its rump in the air and bounce around. It will also wag its tail to indicate to other wolves it is in a mood for play.

121

WOLF SPECIES:
PAST & PRESENT

CHAPTER THREE

WOLF SPECIES: PAST & PRESENT

Once upon a time, wolves covered every corner of the world. Unlike the fairy tales that often begin this way, the wolf's story is still waiting on its "happily ever after" ending. While it may be too late to save some subspecies of wolf from decline, others survive today and thrive owing to careful conservation programs.

Most biologists agree that there are only two core species of wolf in the world today—the gray wolf and the red wolf. However, the scientific community has recently recognized the Abyssinian wolf (*Canis simensis*) that lives exclusively on the highlands of Ethiopia as possibly a third species of wolf. Genetic testing has proved that the Abyssinian wolf is in fact a wolf and not a jackal as was previously believed.

THE GRAY WOLF (*Canis lupus*)

With the scientific name of *Canis lupus*, the gray wolf is known by a number of common names including the timber or western wolf. Regardless of the name it goes by, the gray wolf is the largest wild member of the Canid family and the most common type of wolf in the world.

It inhabits vast expanses of terrain within the northern hemisphere as well as some areas found south of the Equator. With the exception of the lion and the human being, this highly adaptable species once had the largest distribution of any land mammal. Today, the gray wolf can be found in the arctic tundra, coastal areas, tropical rainforests, expansive prairies, forests, and plains of the world. However, despite being found across such a large area, the numbers remain relatively small compared with those in the past.

SUBSPECIES OF THE GRAY WOLF

As with any scientific research, there can some disagreement. In the case of the wolf there is argument over how many subspecies of wolf exist. According to studies, the number and type of subspecies currently named may be inaccurate. It appears that some may have been classifed from a sample that is too small to verify. Furthermore, the overlapping of territorial ranges could have led to the interbreeding among subspecies, causing confusion over which

ABOVE & RIGHT: The gray wolf is the largest of the Canid family and the most prolific.

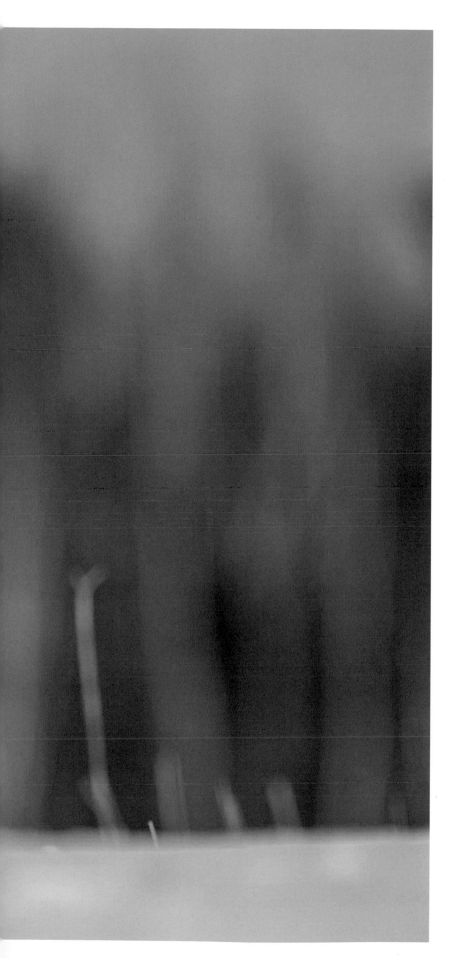

subspecies is which. This may mean that some subspecies are so close in their characteristics that they cannot be clearly defined. In actuality, these hybrids should be classified as such and not as separate subspecies. Today, however, on the positive side, scientists are starting to find it easier to differentiate between subspecies by genetic testing and sequencing.

Despite this contraversy, there are about 30 recognized subspecies of gray wolf known to the world today. The majority of these subspecies are in North America. Interestingly, there is also a line of thought that suggests the domestic dog (*Canis lupus familiaris*) should be reclassified as a new subspecies of gray wolf.

NORTH AMERICAN SUBSPECIES OF GRAY WOLF

1. ARCTIC WOLF (*Canis lupus arctos*)

This subspecies of the gray wolf is one of the most diverse and unique. Also called the winter wolf, polar wolf, white wolf, and snow wolf, this beautiful creature lives in the arctic tundra areas of northern Canada, Greenland, and Alaska. It is the only subspecies of gray wolf that is still found over its entire historic range. This is likely due to its limited interactions with humans in its less than hospitable home habitat of cold, snow, and ice.

Like other gray wolves, the Arctic wolf mainly hunts mammals that it share its frozen home with. The prey it hunts include caribou, musk ox, and the Arctic hare among them. They can go for days without eating anything and when they do eat, can eat up to 20 pounds of meat at a time. With 42 strong teeth, these winter warriors make light work of eating large kills. The teeth are used to break and grind the bones of their prey.

Unlike other gray wolves, the Arctic wolf is specially adapted to survive in the extreme subzero temperatures of the Arctic. It can tolerate the long dark winters in the ice-covered regions it inhabits. The Arctic wolf has specially adapted small ears that help to reduce the surface area from which body heat can be lost. Their paws are thickly padded, furry, and wider than the paws of other gray wolves. This adaptation allows them to get a good grip on the ice and walk on top of the snow. Another feature unique to the Arctic wolf is its brown eyes. This helps to cut down on the glare from the snow.

LEFT: The gray wolf was virtually wiped out in the United States. Today, numbers are recovering.

The most arresting adaptive feature of the Arctic wolf is its striking coat. To help keep it warm, the Arctic wolf has two layers of fur both of which are heavily insulated. The inner layer of fur is short and fuzzy and helps to keep water and moisture out while keeping body heat in. The outer layer is the most striking, unique, and important feature of the Arctic wolf's coat. Most often, the Arctic wolf is white although some are slightly gray, yellow, or brown in color. The white, or off-white colored fur, allows it to blend into its surroundings for protection. It also provides the animal with camouflage when hunting. The Arctic wolf has few predators in its wilderness habitat. The only ones they have to fear are polar bears and people.

These wolves are smaller than many of their cousins. Their overall length is between 3 feet to 6 feet and their weight is between 75 to 125 pounds. The Arctic wolf has an extremely large territory of 1,000 square miles or more and they are highly protective of it. The size of their range is related to the availability of prey in the area.

ABOVE & RIGHT: In the wild, Arctic wolves are prolific hunters. They prey on a variety of creatures including lemmings, reindeer, musk ox, Arctic foxes, birds, insects, and other things.

2. ALASKAN TUNDRA WOLF (*Canis lupus tundrarum*)

Another subspecies of the gray wolf that roams the frozen tundra of the Arctic area of North America is the Alaskan tundra wolf. Also known as the barren-ground wolf, its range is quite literally the barren ground of the frigid regions along the Alaskan coast from the Arctic Archipelago south toward Hudson Bay and westward to the region near Point Barrow. Gerrit Smith Mille, an American botanist and zoologist, identified this subspecies of the gray wolf in 1912.

BELOW: Arctic wolves.

There are several experts who argue against the Alaskan tundra wolf as a separate subspecies of the gray wolf. Some claim that it could possibly be the same animal as either the Mackenzie Valley wolf or the Mackenzie tundra wolf. Others argue that the Alaskan tundra wolf is merely an extension of the interior Alaskan wolf. Despite sharing several characteristics with all three of these subspecies, the Alaskan tundra wolf continues to be considered by the majority of experts as a legitimate subspecies of the gray wolf.

This beautiful creature is a rather large specimen of the wolf. It has a beautiful coat that varies from nearly white to black. Male

Alaskan tundra wolves vary in weight from 85 to 176 pounds; while females range from 80 to 120 pounds. Moreover, some males of this subspecies have been known to reach 220 pounds. In addition, the average Alaskan tundra wolf adult is generally at least six feet in length from the end of its tail to its nose.

Another defining characteristic is that this wolf has a denser dentition than some of the other gray wolf subspecies. This is the arrangement, number, and type of teeth in an animal or human. Like the Arctic wolf, this wolf eats its entire kill; bones and all. These hunters take down large hoofed animals such as deer and even the occasional caribou or musk ox. Like other wolves, the Alaskan tundra wolf is a natural born hunter that chases, seizes, and takes down their

LEFT & BELOW: The Alaskan tundra wolf is a subspecies of gray wolf native to the barren grounds of the Arctic and coastal tundra region from near Point Barrow eastward toward Hudson Bay.

prey. In the absence of larger animals however, the Alaskan tundra wolf will feed on smaller mammals and even vegetation if necessary.

3. ALEXANDER ARCHIPELAGO WOLF
(Canis lupus ligoni)

This striking wolf makes its home along the southern coast of Alaska. They are found on the mainland coast of Alaska from Yakutat Bay to Dixon Entrance. It is quite fascinating that this subspecies is known to swim between the islands in the Alexander Archipelago. In fact, due to its swimming abilities, it can be found on all of the major islands in the archipelago except for three. These densely forested islands are little more than the tops of submerged coastal mountains. They have steep rugged shorelines. Nevertheless, the islands contain an abundance of wildlife for the Alexander Archipelago wolf to eat. Its diet includes moose, beaver, birds, and smaller mammals. It will also eat crabs, clams, salmon, and other oceanic tidbits as it forages around

the coastlines of the islands. However, the favorite prey of the Alexander Archipelago wolf is the Sitka black-tailed deer that live alongside it in its territory.

In 1937, taxonomist Edward Goldman classified the Alexander Archipelago wolf as a subspecies of the gray wolf. At that time, he described them as having darker, coarser, and shorter hair than other northern wolves and also as being smaller. On average, the Alexander Archipelago wolf weighs between 30 and 50 pounds, is roughly 3 to 4 feet in length, and approximately 2 feet tall at its head.

These smaller cousins of the gray wolf live in relative seclusion from other wolf packs due to the natural barriers created by the mountains and the sea. Consequently, their ranges tend to shift significantly over time since there is little concern over intrusion into a larger wolf's territory. Due to the remoteness of its habitat, the Alexander Archipelago wolf is difficult to accurately study and track by researchers who also find population surveys a challenge. However, recent research suggests there are between 750 animals and 1,100 animals.

Since the 1940s, the Alexander Archipelago wolf has had to endure repeated persecution by man. In that time, they have survived the federally sponsored aerial shooting and poisoning campaign that came after World War II. They endured continued bounty payments and aerial shooting throughout the 1960s and into the 1970s. They even withstood the continued persecution by private hunters during the 1980s and early 1990s.

Disappointingly though, in January 2016, the Alexander Archipelago wolf was denied federal protection by the US Fish and Wildlife Service.

4. BAFFIN ISLAND WOLF (*Canis lupus manningi*)

The lauded zoologist Rudolph Martin Anderson was the first to recognize the Baffin Island wolf as a distinct subspecies in 1943. It was named for another zoologist, Thomas Henry Manning, who mapped Baffin Island.

Baffin Island is located in the Baffin Sea between Greenland and Nunavut in Canada. It is ranked the fifth largest island in the world based on size, with nearly 200,000 square miles of land mass. The Baffin Island wolf is found almost exclusively on this island, but is also found on a few small islands adjacent to it.

Smallest of all of the Arctic wolves, the adult Baffin Island wolf reaches an average height of two and a half feet at the shoulder. It weighs a mere 30 to 50 pounds on average and is roughly 3 feet long, including its tail. Its coat is light in color and sometimes white, similar to that of its cousin, the Arctic wolf.

The Baffin Island wolf is perfectly camouflaged to blend into the snowy backdrop of northern Alaska, and consequently it is well

ABOVE: The Alexander Archipelago wolf usually has a darker and shorter coat than the gray wolf.

adapted to hunting. Unlike most wolves, these small wolves are not as carnivorous as other subspecies. Perhaps an evolutionary feature developed due to a limited source of meat, the Baffin Island wolf is an omnivore and thus eats all sorts of plants as well as meat. In fact, they are reported to eat nearly everything edible.

When hunting, the Baffin Island wolf differs from the majority of gray wolves in that it prefers to hunt alone rather than in a pack. At most, they have been seen hunting with one other pack member and this is usually one of the opposite gender.

Although there no is official data relating to their numbers in the wild, Baffin Island wolves are believed to be endangered.

5. BERNARD'S WOLF (*Canis lupus bernardi*)
EXTINCT

Rudolph Martin Anderson, acclaimed zoologist and explorer, identified the Bernard's wolf in 1943. Also called the Bank's Island wolf, Victoria's Island wolf, and the Bank's Island tundra wolf, this Canadian subspecies of gray wolf was named after Peter Bernard who with his nephew Joseph made their living hunting wolves. Bernard and his family did their best to wipe out the Bernard's wolf and as a consequence of their hunting, the subspecies was completely eradicated from the the Victoria archipelago, by 1952. After that, it was found only on Bank's Island. This moderately-sized island, rests north of the Canadian mainland in the Arctic Ocean.

The Bernard's wolf grew to be up to four feet tall and weighed between 60 to 110 pounds. They could measure six feet long from tip to tip (from the tip of the nose to the tip of the tail).

This large specimen of the Arctic region was known for its unique fur. It had long, nearly white fur, with a black stripe down its spine. Consequently, pelts were highly sought-after by fur traders. By 1993, there was no sign of the Bernard's wolf anywhere within its known territory and it is now believed to have gone extinct.

6. BRITISH COLUMBIAN WOLF (*Canis lupus columbianus*)

In 1941, Major Edward Goldman, senior biologist for the Division of Wilderness Research at the US Fish and Wildlife Service, classified the British Columbian wolf as a subspecies of the gray wolf. While it was once found across the majority of British Columbia, Alberta, southwestern Alaska, and portions of Yukon, its historic territories intersected with those of the Cascade Mountain wolf and the Alexander Archipelago wolf. Today, it is found in just a few areas of its former range.

This northern wolf shares traits with both the Mackenzie Valley wolf and the Alaskan interior wolf but is smaller. However, it is still one of the larger gray wolf subspecies. The British Columbian wolf

ABOVE: The Baffin Island wolf is the smallest of the Arctic wolves.

weighs on average between 80 and 150 pounds. Furthermore, it is nearly six feet from nose to rump. The British Columbian wolf is often black in color with gray or brown mottles throughout its long coat. Similar to other wolves of this region, the British Columbian wolf feeds on large hoofed mammals, hares, and even birds. Efforts are currently underway to protect this subspecies.

LEFT & ABOVE: The Eastern timber wolf is particularly susceptible to hybridization. Genetically, it has a close relationship with the coyote and therefore able to breed with it.

7. CASCADE MOUNTAIN WOLF (*Canis lupus fuscus*)
EXTINCT

This medium-sized wolf was also known as the brown wolf. Sir John Richardson, a Scottish surgeon and arctic explorer, recognized the Cascade mountain wolf as a gray wolf subspecies in 1839.

The Cascade mountain wolf had a striking coat of grayish-brown which occasionally would have had a touch of red or black in it. It stood only 3 feet tall at the shoulder, weighed 85 pounds on average, and was 4 to 5 feet long.

It was once found throughout the Cascade mountains from northern California up to southwestern Canada. Settler hostility coupled with government-sponsored bounties brought about the extinction of the Cascade mountain wolf by 1940, a century after it was first recognized.

8. EASTERN TIMBER WOLF (*Canis lupus lycaon*)

Sometimes referred to as the eastern wolf, this was the first subspecies of gray wolf identified in North America all the way back in 1775.

It is interesting to note that scientific studies conducted in recent years have suggested that the eastern timber wolf is actually its own distinct species of wolf, *Canis lycaon*. However, as of 2018 no official change in its classification had been made.

Eastern timber wolves come in an assortment of colors. Most look similar to the domestic Husky with multi-colored coats. The coat has a base color of brown and gray with markings of white, gray, and black across the back. Often, its lower legs and muzzle can be tinged with brownish-red.

Smaller than their cousin the gray wolf, the eastern timber wolf weighs between 50 and 100 pounds. The average adult male specimen weighs in at 75 pounds with the average adult female weighing slightly less at roughly 60 pounds. Up to two and a half feet tall at the shoulder, this majestic creature measures up to five and a half feet long from tip to tip.

The eastern timber wolf once roamed vast ranges across North America. From the northern territories of Ontario, Manitoba, and Quebec in Canada, all the way down to northeastern Florida in the United States, the eastern timber wolf cut a latitudinal swath that stretched from the Atlantic Ocean to central Minnesota. Today, as with all other wolves, that historic range has been severely reduced. The eastern timber wolf maintains more than 40 percent of its original Canadian range, with the greatest concentration found in the Algonquin Park of Ontario. However, nearly all of the specimens that once roamed the United States have long since disappeared, with the eastern timber wolf now occupying only three percent of its total former range.

Mainly found today in the St. Lawrence River and Great Lakes areas of southeast Ontario and southwest Quebec, the eastern timber wolf has learned to avoid human activity and thus, makes its home in remote, densely forested areas that are sparsely populated by humans.

The territory size of an eastern timber wolf pack can be highly variable. This depends largely on the availability of food. Ranging anywhere from 20 to 120 square miles in size, each territory is fiercely defended from intrusions by other packs.

Despite its efforts to avoid humans, our activity is still the greatest threat to the eastern timber wolf today. They are listed as endangered

LEFT: A juvenile eastern timber wolf.

ABOVE RIGHT: The eastern timber wolf has many coat color variations.

within every US state of its historic range, except for Minnesota where the population has climbed to the "threatened" status.

Numbers continue to climb for this wolf—a positive sign considering it nearly went extinct at the turn of the twentieth century.

9. GREAT PLAINS WOLF (*Canis lupus nubilus*)

The Great Plains wolf is also called the buffalo wolf. It is the most common gray wolf subspecies in the lower 48 contiguous United States. Thomas Say, known as the father of descriptive entomology, inaccurately labeled the Great Plains wolf as a separate species, *Canis nubilus* in 1823. Eighteen years later in 1941, German naturalist and explorer, Prince Maximilian of Wied-Neuwied reclassified the wolf as a subspecies of the gray wolf.

At one time, when numbers were much higher, the Great Plains wolf had the largest range of any North American subspecies. This historic range stretched across the majority of central and northeastern

Canada, the western United States, and southeastern Alaska. Yet, the Great Plains wolf nearly met with extinction in the United States by the 1930s. In fact, in 1926 it was added to the list of extinct wolves.

However, studies showed not long after that, that the packs found in Upper Michigan, Minnesota, and Wisconsin were indeed Great Plains wolves. Still, by the mid-1960s, only a few of these once prolific animals survived on the border of Ontario and Minnesota. The modern range for the Great Plains wolf today stretches across Ontario, Wisconsin, Minnesota, and Upper Michigan.

The Great Plains wolf varies widely in length from four to more than six feet from tip to tip. They weigh between 60 and 110 pounds and are often 3 to 4 feet tall at the head. The female Great Plains wolf is more or less 80 percent the size of the male. The coat of this wolf is usually a blend of two or more colors that may be black, buff, red, gray, and brown.

For the most part, the mating and reproduction cycles of the Great Plains wolf are the same as for most other wolves. Only the alpha pair reproduce. Females gestate for 63 days. The litters consist of four to six pups born in a birthing den. One interesting variation in the Great Plain wolf's breeding cycle is that it has a shortened mating season. This subspecies becomes fully grown in six to eight months and is sexually mature by about 22 months.

In 1974, the Great Plains wolf was added to the Endangered Species List and given federal protection. This likely saved them from complete extinction. Federal protection was a relative success, as four years later in 1978, this wolf species was reclassified as just threatened. By 2009, the number of Great Plains wolves in the Great Lakes region had climbed to more than 4,000. As a result, the United

BELOW: A dark-coated eastern timber wolf.

States Fish and Wildlife Service removed it from the Endangered Species List. This prompted a lawsuit filed against the agency by five animal protection groups demanding the Great Plains wolf be put back under federal protection. The courts agreed.

ABOVE: The Great Plains wolf is a large good-looking animal. After near extinction, it is now doing well in the Great Plains region of America.

10. GREENLAND WOLF (*Canis lupus orion*) EXTINCT

The Greenland wolf is listed as extinct here for the simple reason that there are none in the world today. That may seem like simple logic and an unnecessary explanation of the meaning of "extinct," however, rest assured it is not. Considering the Greenland wolf is one of the most highly contended subspecies classifications among gray wolves, the designation of extinct becomes less exact. In essence, if the Greenland wolf ever existed, it is extinct now.

The question that arises over this animal stems from the belief that it is, in fact, simply a migrating population of the Arctic wolf and not a subspecies at all. The classification of the Greenland wolf as a distinct subspecies of gray wolf came in 1935. Reginald Innes Pocock, a British zoologist best known for identifying and classifying spiders, stepped outside his comfort zone to classify this wolf as its own subspecies.

Pocock described the Greenland wolf as having a coat of white fur that is quite similar to that of the Arctic wolf but being of smaller stature. However, aside from this description and Pocock's notes regarding the animal, there is no available evidence to suggest that the Greenland wolf ever existed as a unique subspecies with distinct subspecies characteristics.

In fact, the one feature that separates the Greenland wolf from the Arctic wolf is its smaller size. A factor that is more likely due to malnutrition than any morphological difference between *Canis lupus orion* and *Canis lupus arctos*. These two wolves are identical heights and lengths with weight being the only foreseeable difference between them.

Consequently, the majority of zoologists and other scientists involved in the classification of animals believe that the Greenland wolf is simply an off-shoot of the Arctic wolf that migrated across the icy waters that separate Canada and Greenland. Sightings of wolves on the sea ice located in the Nares Strait, part of the Baffin Bay, seem to suggest that this migration is still occurring today.

If there ever was a Greenland wolf, it is extinct now and it left us no proof of its existence other than the notes and claims of one scientist who only began studying mammals at the end of his career.

11. HUDSON BAY WOLF – (*Canis lupus hudsonicus*)

Biologist Edward Goldman classified the Hudson Bay wolf as a

unique subspecies of gray wolf in 1941. It is also known by the name it was called before this, the tundra wolf.

Native to Canada, the historical range of this medium-sized wolf remains largely intact. Found west of the Hudson Bay and extending north from upper Manitoba throughout the Northwest Territories and above, these apex predators will occasionally be found migrating farther south with the caribou herds that are its primary food source.

With average body lengths of four and a half feet and heights up to three feet at the shoulder, the Hudson Bay wolf is a moderately-sized subspecies. As is often the case, females are slightly smaller than their male counterparts. These wolves generally weigh between 80 and 140 pounds. Their coats are bushy and vary from a yellowish

BELOW & RIGHT: The Hudson Bay wolf is native to Canada.

cream color to a light gray, growing lighter in the winter to help with camouflage.

Like most of their lupine cousins, the Hudson Bay wolf lives and hunts in packs. This makes it easier for them to feed on the large hoofed animals of their home range. Uniquely, in times when prey is scarce, the Hudson Bay wolf will feed on carrion (the decaying flesh of dead animals) like a scavenger.

The Hudson Bay wolf's population has never been evaluated by the International Union for Conservation of Nature (IUCN) for Red List consideration. Similarly, it does not fall under the United States' Endangered Species List either. However, most researchers and scientists consider it to be endangered.

12. INTERIOR ALASKAN WOLF (*Canis lupus pambasileus*)

In 1905, the wolf commonly called the Yukon wolf was officially classified as a subspecies of gray wolf and dubbed the interior Alaskan wolf by zoologist Daniel Elliot. However, there is still some debate about whether or not it is in reality a separate subspecies or rather simply an extension of the Alaskan tundra wolf.

In terms of physical appearance, this wolf is the largest wolf in North America and quite possibly the world. Reaching a whopping seven feet in length from tip to tip, the interior Alaskan wolf is so large that it exceeds the standard size for a wolf species. Roughly four feet tall at the shoulder and reaching a weight of between 85 and 155 pounds, this subspecies is indeed a fierce looking predator.

With its dark coat of black or near black, images of this impressive wolf are reminiscent of the Dire Wolf of the last epoch. Gray, brown, or white markings provide some relief to the dark backdrop of its coat.

The interior Alaskan wolf has populations throughout the interior of the Canadian Yukon and Alaska. However, it is curiously absent from the tundra region of the arctic coast. Possibly, this is due to competion with the interior Alaskan wolf that also lives in this region.

13. KENAI PENINSULA WOLF (*Canis lupus alces*)
EXTINCT

Major Edward Goldman, senior biologist for the Division of Wilderness Research at the US Fish and Wildlife Service, identified the Kenai Peninsula wolf as a distinct subspecies of gray wolf in 1941.

LEFT & BELOW: The Hudson Bay wolf is a subspecies of the gray wolf.

This identification was based entirely on skeletal findings. Based on these findings, the Kenai Peninsula wolf stood four feet tall at the shoulder and was an average of six feet long from tip to tip. At an average of 200 pounds, this wolf far surpassed any other in the area.

Until driven to extinction by man, the Kenai Peninsula wolf was the largest wolf in North America. They lived on the Kenai Peninsula of Alaska and the surrounding areas. The Kenai Peninsula itself is a large chunk of land that extends from the coast of southcentral Alaska, just below Anchorage. It is saved from being an island by a narrow swath of land that connects it to the mainland. It is surrounded by the frigid waters of the Gulf of Alaska and Cook Inlet.

In the late 1890s, the wolf population of the Kenai Peninsula was bountiful. Unfortunately for them, gold was found there around that time and the gold rush brought prospectors, settlers, and other humans to the area. By 1915, so called predator control programs had nearly wiped out the Kenai Peninsula wolf. With continued hunting, trapping, and poisoning they were gone entirely by 1925.

14. LABRADOR WOLF (*Canis lupus labradorius*)

Another wolf identified by biologist Edward Goldman, the Labrador wolf was added as a subspecies of gray wolf in 1937. Living in the vast, remote, and rugged landscape of Canada, this elusive wolf is one of the least studied or photographed wolves in the world.

Unlike other wolves, the Labrador wolf still inhabits the majority of its historic range in the northern Quebec and Labrador areas of Canada. A drop in their population in the middle of the twentieth century gave rise to the largest herd of caribou in the world. So large, in fact, that it helped the population of Labrador wolves to recover afterwards. Not surprisingly, the caribou is the Labrador wolf's main food source. However, like other wolves, when caribou numbers are low, they will hunt and eat other species within their territory.

Similar in size to an eastern timber wolf, the Labrador wolf ranges from four and half to six feet in length. The average specimen weighs between 75 and 140 pounds. It has a dark gray to off-white coat.

They are classified as endangered by the Canadian government.

15. MACKENZIE VALLEY WOLF (*Canis lupus occidentalis*)

Sir John Richardson classified the Mackenzie Valley wolf as a gray wolf subspecies in 1829. It is also known by the names Mackenzie tundra wolf, Alaskan timber wolf, Canadian timber wolf, Manitoba wolf, and other localized names.

The Mackenzie Valley wolf inhabits much of its historic range throughout the majority of western Canada and Alaska. This includes Unimak Island which is the largest of the Aleutian Islands.

In 1995, a number of Mackenzie Valley wolves were caged and brought south in an effort to reintroduce wolves to the Yellowstone National Park and central Idaho. However, this program had limited success, as after a while the pack sizes of the newly introduced wolves suffered. Mackenzie Valley wolf packs usually have up to 12 members but sometimes as many as 30. Their territories average around 600 square miles. However, in the new areas where the Mackenzie Valley wolves were moved, the maximum pack size was just ten individuals per pack in both Idaho and Yellowstone.

Mackenzie Valley wolves are roughly three feet tall at the shoulder and six feet long from tip to tip on average. They are heavy wolves with the average male weighing between 100 and 145 pounds,

RIGHT: A large subspecies of wolf, the interior Alaskan is an impressive animal. Its looks are reminiscent of the extinct Dire Wolf.

the females being roughly 15 percent lighter. Interestingly, the *Guinness Book of Animal World Records* claims that one Mackenzie Valley wolf weighed a whopping 230 pounds and was deemed the heaviest wolf ever recorded.

It is not surprising that these wolves are so large. With an abundant availability of food in the territories where they live, these wolves grow into large, healthy specimens. The Mackenzie Valley wolf is a prolific hunter. Its diet includes salmon, snowshoe hare, ground squirrel, mountain goat, sheep, musk ox, elk, wood bison, caribou, mouse, deer, beaver, vole, and lemming.

LEFT: The Labrador wolf inhabits the northern Quebec and Labrador areas of Canada.

ABOVE and PAGE 152: The Mackenzie Valley wolf inhabits areas of Alaska; the upper Mackenzie River Valley; southward into the Canadian provinces of British Columbia, Alberta, and Saskatchewan; as well as the northwestern United States.

As with other wolves, humans are the greatest threat to the Mackenzie Valley wolf. However, conservation efforts have allowed the population to grow to more than 10,000 individuals and counting. The US Fish and Wildlife Service has even attempted to remove this wolf from the endangered list for the western Great Lakes and Northern Rockies. However, this has met with opposition.

16. MEXICAN GRAY WOLF (*Canis lupus baileyi*)

The Mexican gray wolf, also known as the Mexican lobo, has the distinction of being one of the few creatures to go extinct in the wild yet make a comeback. It is fitting that the Mexican gray wolf returned through the efforts of people since it was the efforts of people that caused it to disappear in the first place.

The Mexican gray wolf is the smallest subspecies of gray wolf in North America. Ranging from four to slightly more than five feet in length from its nose to the base of its tail, this little wolf stands just two and a half feet high at the shoulder. It weighs from 50 to 90 pounds.

The coat of this gray wolf subspecies is a blend of rust, cream, black, and gray. The Mexican gray wolf, is roughly the same size and stature as the German Shepherd dog and slightly similar in its markings and color.

This wolf once lived throughout Mexico, hence the name. Its territory was the remote mountain forests, scrublands, and grasslands of Mexico and the American states of New Mexico, Arizona, and the western edge of the state of Texas. Like many of its lupine cousins, the Mexican gray wolf ran afoul of settlers at the turn of the twentieth century.

In a familiar story, the settlers encroached into this wolf's historic range and began hunting the wolf's natural prey. The caused a disturbance to the delicate ecosystem of the area and a food shortage for the wolves. In order to survive, the wolves to began feeding on the livestock that the settlers had brought with them. As a consequence, the wolves then became a target for hunters.

Mexican gray wolves behave in a similar fashion to other wolves. They will initiate play by bouncing and wagging their tails, howl to communicate and warn off outsiders, and use urine to mark their territories. They are highly social and loyal to their pack.

The Mexican gray wolf's mating cycle and pup rearing mimics that of other wolves. The alphas reproduce and then the pack helps raise the pups. When the pups reach sexual maturity they will either join their familial pack or strike out on their own in the hope of starting their own pack.

Wolves are opportunistic feeders. They will eat whatever is available around them rather than go hungry. For the Mexican gray wolf, this includes wild pigs, antelope, small deer, rabbits, and rodents. In addition, they will eat the many lizards and insects that are found in the hotter climates.

BELOW & OVERLEAF: The Mexican gray wolf has had a difficult past. It was extinct in the wild. However, with conservation efforts, it has been released back into the wild and numbers are growing.

The Mexican gray wolf is considered the most endangered species in North America. This is despite a successful conservation program and reintroduction effort which saved it from the brink of extinction. In fact, the Mexican gray wolf was extinct in the wild with only four specimens alive in captivity when it was finally realized the species needed help to survive. Today, there are roughly 60 individuals living in the wild and more than 300 in zoos across North America. While their numbers are slowly growing, they remain protected by both the United States and Mexican governments.

17. MOGOLLON MOUNTAIN WOLF (*Canis lupus mogollonensis*) EXTINCT

In 1937, biologist Edward Goldman, senior biologist for the Division of Wilderness Research at the US Fish and Wildlife Service classified the Mogollon mountain wolf as a gray wolf subspecies. This wolf is also known as the southwestern wolf or simply the Mogollon wolf. It was named after the Mogollon Mountains that stretch from southeast New Mexico to the Sacramento Mountains in central New Mexico. It was a medium-sized wolf, larger than the Mexican gray wolf but smaller than the Texas wolf.

By 1935, two years before its classification as a gray wolf subspecies, the Mogollon mountain wolf had been driven to extinction, never to be seen again.

18. NEWFOUNDLAND WOLF (*Canis lupus beothucus*) EXTINCT

The Newfoundland wolf was formally described as a subspecies of gray wolf by zoologists Thomas Barbour and G.M. Allen in 1937.

BELOW & RIGHT: Mexican gray wolf.

This was seven years after it became officially extinct (unofficially the last one was shot in 1911). The wolf was named after a tribe of people called the Beothuk who were declared extinct in 1829. They too, like the Newfoundland wolf, were previous residents of Newfoundland.

Prior to extinction, Newfoundland was the sole island home of the Newfoundland wolf. It was five and a half feet in length from tip to tip and weighed up to a hundred pounds. It is believed that its coat was white with a black stripe down its spine.

While predator control methods, including trapping and hunting did their part to speed along the extinction of the Newfoundland wolf, the greatest reason for its downfall was a sudden food shortage around

the turn of the 20th century. At the time, the Newfoundland wolf's main food supply was the caribou, which was also suffering from over-hunting as well as disease. When the population of caribou dropped drastically in the early 1900s most of the remaining wolves starved to death. Not to be outdone by natural selection, man struck the final blow with the last wolf being shot after capture in 1911.

19. NORTHERN ROCKY MOUNTAIN WOLF (*Canis lupus irremotus*)

A prolific classifier of gray wolf subspecies, Major Edward Goldman identified the Northern Rocky Mountain wolf in 1937. Originally, this wolf's habitat began in southern Alberta and stretched to the end of the Northern Rocky Mountains. Early records show that the Northern Rocky Mountain wolf roamed many of the forests that would later become known as Yellowstone National Park.

The Rocky Mountain wolf is of moderate size, and weighs an average of 80 to 115 pounds. It is five feet from tip to tip. It is a lighter colored animal than its southern cousin was, the extinct Southern Rocky Mountain wolf. Its coat includes far more white than black.

LEFT & BELOW: Unlike its extinct cousin, the Northern Rocky Mountain wolf is holding its own and is no longer critically endangered.

In some locations the Northen Rocky Mountain wolf has been removed from the endangered list as quotas for the species are considered stable.

20. SOUTHERN ROCKY MOUNTAIN WOLF (*Canis lupus youngi*) EXTINCT

Like its northern cousin, the Southern Rocky Mountain wolf was classified as a gray wolf subspecies in 1937 by biologist Edward Goldman. Its scientific name *youngi* is meant to honor Stanley P. Young who oversaw the extermination of the wolf for the United States government. This may seem morbid and distasteful now but at

the time he was lauded as a great hero for successfully eradicating the villainous wolf.

Once, these wolves roamed throughout the northern Utah and the southern Wyoming regions of the Rocky Mountains and south through western Colorado and into northern Arizona and New Mexico. Before they were eradicated they even spread into central Nevada and southern California. They resembled a large Northern Rocky Mountain wolf in size, stretching to over five feet long and averaging 125 pounds. Their fur was a light buff much like that of the Great Plains wolf.

In 1935, excessive poisoning, trapping, and hunting of this wolf led to the Southern Rocky Mountain wolf's extinction.

21. TEXAS WOLF (*Canis lupus montrabilis*) EXTINCT

The Texan wolf was another 1937 addition to the gray wolf subspecies list by senior biologist Edward Goldman at the Division of Wilderness Research at the US Fish and Wildlife Service. It once roamed throughout central Texas, southeastern New Mexico, and along the border of Mexico into Louisiana. Smaller than other wolves of the area, yet not as small as the Mexican gray wolf, they were generally dark in color although some specimens were nearly white.

In 1942, just five years after being recognized as a distinct subspecies of gray wolf, the Texas wolf became extinct.

22. VANCOUVER ISLAND WOLF (*Canis lupus crassodon*)

In 1932, Dr. E. Raymond Hall, considered one of the nation's leading authorities in the field of natural history, identified the Vancouver Island wolf as a subspecies of gray wolf. These Canadian wolves retain the majority of their historic range on Vancouver Island despite nearly going extinct in the early 1970s.

Vancouver Island lies off the shore of Canada in the province of British Columbia and bears the distinction of being the largest island off the west coast of North America. Unlike much of Canada, this island has moderate temperatures and lush forests. Thus, the Vancouver Island wolf bears physical characteristics that suit its environment.

These are moderately-sized animals, most often under three feet tall at the shoulder and four feet from tip to tip. The Vancouver Island wolf weighs between 65 and 90 pounds. Its coat is a mixture of black, brown, and gray (unlike the Arctic wolf that is lighter in color).

The primary prey of these apex predators include the Roosevelt elk, Columbian black-tailed deer, and eastern cottontail rabbit. They also feed on salmon, crabs, and other oceanic creatures.

In 1970, the Canadian Wildlife Federations added the Vancouver Island wolf to its Endangered Wildlife in Canada list. As part of the

conservation effort, a counting/sighting program was established on Vancouver Island with the initial count in 1973 being 37 individuals. Three years later, the effort to save the Vancouver Island wolf seemed to be working as that number climbed to 88. Within another four years, the population of Vancouver Island wolves reached a point where it could be formally removed from the endangered list.

ABOVE: A Vancouver Island wolf in captivity. It is very social with other wolves. In the wild, it lives in packs of about five to thirty-five. It is very shy and rarely seen by humans.

SUBSPECIES OF GRAY WOLF IN THE REST OF THE WORLD

While North America has by far more subspecies of gray wolf than in any other part of the world, they are also found in many other countries.

1. ARABIAN WOLF (*Canis lupus arabs*)

The Arabian wolf can be found in countries throughout the Middle East including northwestern Egypt, Saudi Arabia, Jordan, Yemen, Oman, Iraq, and Israel. Even though it is the largest canid in the region, it is the smallest subspecies of the gray wolves. The Arabian wolf stands at two feet tall at the shoulder and weighs of average of 40 pounds. Its light brownish-gray coat is short. The ears of the Arabian wolf are large for its head. In the searing heat of the Middle East, this adaptation helps it to regulate its body temperature by losing excess heat through its ears. Another interesting adaptation is that it is known to dig out a burrow in the sand to protect itself from the sun when it is at its hottest.

The Arabian wolf is renowned for its bright yellow eyes. This is a unique genetic trait that many other subspecies of wolf also possess. However, when an Arabian wolf is discovered with brown eyes, this reveals an impure bloodline, which is most likely due to interbreeding with feral dogs.

Unlike other gray wolves, Arabian wolves only form packs during their October through December mating season. This unusual

BELOW: The Arabian wolf is a subspecies of gray wolf which lives in parts of the Middle East. This small wolf is adapted to desert conditions. It eats small and medium-sized prey as well as carrion, plants, and garbage.

behavior is likely due to a scarcity of food throughout the majority of the year. The Arabian wolf's diet consists of small birds, insects, reptiles, rodents, and mammals up to the size of a goat. In addition, it will feed on carrion, plants, fruits, and garbage in times when meat is scarce.

In some areas of its historic range, the Arabian wolf has disappeared completely and in other places it is endangered. Natural recovery for this species is particularly difficult in the wild. The standard smaller litter size of only two or three pups prevents numbers from easily rising.

2. CASPIAN SEA WOLF (*Canis lupus campestris*)

Russian scientist Ivan Dwigubski classified the Caspian Sea wolf as a gray wolf sub species in 1804 under the common name of steppe wolf. Others call this majestic creature the caucasian wolf. The Caspian Sea wolf has a short coat in shades of gray blended with

ABOVE: The Caspian Sea wolf's coloration is generally dull gray tinted with other colors.

brown, black, and rust colored hairs scattered across its back. These desert colors help it to blend in with its surroundings. The Caspian Sea wolf is smaller than most gray wolf subspecies, weighing about 88 pounds.

This wolf's historic range includes all the countries that border the Black Sea and the Caspian Sea. After decades of persecution and hunting by humans, the Caspian Sea wolf currently exists only in an isolated area in the outermost southwestern part of Russia that borders the northern half of the Caspian Sea.

The Caspian Sea wolf is a prolific predator that will eat a diverse range of prey. Like other gray wolves, it hunts in packs for large prey. However, unlike the majority of their gray wolf cousins, the Caspian

Sea wolf will also hunt on its own or only with its mate. The prey of choice for these wolves includes rodents, seals, herd animals, and fish. They are also known to eat fruits and berries in times of food scarcity. It has been documented that this capable hunter, in some instances, will hunt and kill more than it is capable of eating. It has been known for it to kill Caspian seals quite wantonly. This habit is quite puzzling as gray wolves largely kill only what they can eat and then gorge themselves after to ensure nothing is wasted. The Caspian Sea wolf however, will at times leave a seal uneaten. Once it has had its fill though, this wolf can go for weeks without eating again.

LEFT: A Caspian Sea wolf is an endangered subspecies of the gray wolf.

BELOW: The endangered Chinese wolf has a vastly reduced habitat.

The author Tim Cope has written about the important relationship between man and the Caspian Sea wolf on the steppe of Russia:

"Perhaps most important for nomads was the belief in the symbiosis that existed between wolf and humans on the steppe. Wolves were an integral part of keeping the balance of nature, ensuring that plagues of rabbits and rodents didn't break out, which in turn protected the all-important pasture for the nomads' herds."
~ Tim Cope, Australian adventurer, author, filmmaker, and more.

Hunted as a nuisance for decades, the Caspian Sea wolf was nearly hunted to extinction. The Mongolian Red List of Mammals, which resembles a program similar to that of UICN Red List, has had the Caspian Sea wolf listed as endangered since 2007.

3. CHINESE WOLF (*Canis lupus chanco*)

Also known as the Himalayan wolf, the Tibetan wolf, and the Mongolian wolf, this subspecies of gray wolf was identified in 1863 by John Edward Gray, a British zoologist.

The territories of the Chinese wolf today are a mere fraction of the historic ranges it once enjoyed. The areas where it still populates include the cold mountainous regions within China, India, Bhutan, Russia, Nepal, and Tibet.

"Reflective of the deep sense of gratitude and respect Mongolians reserved for wolves, there was a belief that only through wolves could the spirit of a deceased human be set free to go to Heaven."
~ Tim Cope, Australian adventurer, author, filmmaker, and more.

Scientific studies of the Chinese wolf are limited. This is due firstly, to its scarcity, and secondly due to the remoteness of where it lives. However, it is known that this elusive wolf lives in packs and has a large range that stretches for hundreds of miles.

Chinese wolves are roughly five and a half feet from tip to tip. They stand a little more than two feet tall at the shoulder and weigh an average of 65 pounds. When compared to the Eurasian wolf which inhabits the same regions, this wolf is a little larger in stature but has shorter legs. Its skull size is comparable to the Eurasian wolf but has a thinner, longer muzzle. The Chinese wolf has a long shaggy coat that gives it a fuzzy, woolly look. Its coat is usually a blend of black, gray, brown, yellow, and white. Chinese wolves live between 6 and 11 years in the wild and as many as 20 years in captivity.

As well as being an outstanding hunter, the Chinese wolf is known to be versatile, too. It will hunt at any time of day or night with proficiency. Furthermore, it can hunt in a pack or alone. Their prey includes blue sheep, deer, and other large hoofed mammals. They will also hunt smaller mammals such as ground squirrels, mice, hares, and marmots.

The Chinese wolf is currently listed as endangered and has been since 1991. It is thought by researchers that the population is at least stable, if not, recovering slightly. Despite its rarity, the Chinese wolf is still viewed as a nuisance by many and is persecuted because of this. It is now considered that without rapid intervention and a proactive conservation effort this could possibly be the next wolf to go extinct.

4. EURASIAN GRAY WOLF (*Canis lupus lupus*)

The first subspecies of gray wolf to be identified, the Eurasian gray wolf is also known as the common gray wolf. Carl Linnaeus, known as the father of modern taxonomy, described the Eurasian gray wolf in his book *Systema Naturae* in 1758.

LEFT & ABOVE: The Eurasian gray wolf is larger than the North American gray wolf. It also has a much more melodious howl.

OVERLEAF: A small pack of Eurasian gray wolves in Norway.

The historic range of this wolf covered most of Asia and Europe. Today, however, it still maintains the largest range of any gray wolf sub species. This range is broadly limited to Western Europe, Scandinavia, Russia, China, Mongolia, and the Himalayan Mountains. Highly adaptable to a wide variety of diverse environs, this size of the Eurasian gray wolf's territory relies strongly on the availability of water and prey.

These wolves are on average 3 feet tall at the shoulder and weigh between 70 and 130 pounds. Their length can vary significantly from

LEFT & ABOVE: The Eurasian gray wolf.

three and a half feet to nearly six feet long from tip to tip. Females are on average 20 percent smaller than males. The Eurasian wolf can be a combination of many colors including black, gray, red, cream, and white.

As with most other gray wolf subspecies, the Eurasian gray wolf hunts in a pack and feeds largely on hoofed herding mammals. They will also eat rodents, fish, fruits, and berries. When prey is scarce, they will hunt alone rather than in a pack.

As always, persecution by humans tops the list of mortality factors for the Eurasian gray wolf. In addition, other factors are also a threat to them. These factors include injuries incurred by prey, killing by other wolves, parasites, diseases, and starvation. Its average lifespan is between seven to ten years in the wild.

Conservation efforts for the Eurasian gray wolf varies widely across its range. However, it is protected in European Union countries.

5. HOKKAIDO WOLF (*Canis lupus hattai*) — EXTINCT
One of Japan's two wolf species, the Hokkaido wolf, was classified as a gray wolf subspecies in 1931 by Japanese zoologist Kyukichi Kishida. It was also known locally as the Ezo wolf in Japan and the Sakhalin wolf in Russia.

The Hokkaido wolf once inhabited the Japanese island of Hokkaido it was named for. It was also found in the Kuril Islands, too. In addition, they were formerly found on the Russian territories of the Kamchatka Peninsula and Sakhalin Island.

Closely resembling the standard gray wolf in height, weight, length, and other physical characteristics, the Hokkaido wolf was usually a tannish gray or pale gray. It fed on the creatures that were found in its habitat. These included birds, deer, and rabbits among other things.

The Hokkaido wolf went extinct in 1889. This was caused by a number of factors including the deliberate poisoning with strychnine by farmers who viewed it as a nuisance, a severe winter in 1878 when heavy snows blanketed their habitat causing them to starve, and a general commitment to their persecution.

6. HONSHU WOLF (*Canis lupus hodophilax*) EXTINCT

In addition to the Hokkaido wolf, the other wolf native to Japan was the Honshu wolf which was officially dubbed the Japanese wolf. Moreover, other names included the mountain dog, the hondo wolf, and the yamainu, which means jackal in Japanese.

Dutch zoologist Coenraad Temminck identified the Honshu wolf as a gray wolf subspecies in 1839. Its historic range covered the Japanese islands of Shikoku, Kyushu, and Honshu, from which it gets its name. Its main territories were remote mountainous areas.

The Honshu wolf held the distinction of being one of the world's smallest wolves. It stood a little over a foot tall at the shoulder and measured less than three feet from tip to tip. In relation to its body, it had shortish legs. The Honshu wolf had a coat of wiry short hairs in dark shades of gray, brown, and black. Its small size, stature and unusual coat prompted the argument that the Honshu was possibly a unique species, that may not even be canid.

Another rare quality of the Honshu wolf was its relationship with human farmers within its range. Rather than the standard animosity between wolves and farmers, these wolves were praised for preying on wild boar, deer, and smaller pests that damaged their crops.

The welcomed Honshu wolf flourished in its home range until 1732, when domestic dogs brought to Japan on trade ships, introduced rabies to the Japanese archipelago. Combined with the deforestation of the wolf's habitat and persecution from humans who did not value the Honshu wolf as much as the local farmers, rabies devastated the population.

However, as the history of wolves has shown, it is man that strikes the last blow in wiping out species of animals. The last known living Honshu wolf was shot in 1905 in a park area on Honshu island.

Sadly, all that remains of this once esteemed wolf are five mounted specimens.

ABOVE & RIGHT: The Iberian wolf has a warm reddish coat that changes with the seasons becoming lighter in summer.

7. IBERIAN WOLF (*Canis lupus signatus*)

Spanish zoologist Angelus Cabrera identified the Iberian wolf in 1907 as a gray wolf subspecies. Despite arguing among taxonomists, biologist Robert Wayne quieted their concerns by conducting genetic testing that confirmed its status as a sub species of gray wolf.

Today, the Iberian wolf can be found in the forests and plains of northwest Spain, the northeastern edge of Portugal, and a scattering of isolated areas in the Sierra Morena mountain range. In better days,

before its persecution, the Iberian wolf was found across the whole of the Iberian Peninsula. However, as the Iberian wolf's range decreased in size, their numbers dropped, too.

These medium-sized wolves have a thinner build than the Eurasian gray wolf. The males of this subspecies weigh up to 90 pounds with females roughly 20 percent smaller. Their coats change with the seasons becoming an ochre or light gray in the warmer season and transitioning to a darker reddish brown during the winter.

Depending on where it lives, the Iberian wolf's diet will vary greatly. Cantabrian wolves hunt wild boar, red deer, and roe deer. The Iberian wolves of Galicia feed on pig and chicken remains from local farms. Those in Castilla y Len are believed to exist largely on rabbits. Unfortunately, for the Iberian wolf and regardless of where it lives,

ABOVE & RIGHT: In some areas where hunting is banned, the Iberian wolf numbers have in increased. In others such as the Sierra Morena mountains it is virtually extinct.

one if its food sources is livestock. Understandably, this has caused friction with farmers, who as a consequence, consider the animal to be a nuisance.

In the 1950s, the Spanish government officially recognized the Iberian wolf as a pest and offered a bounty for dead wolves. This decimated the population to less than 500 individuals. Today, hunting is banned by Portugal and Spain and both countries are now working to conserve this important subspecies. In recent years, the overall

status of the Iberian wolf has been updated from endangered to vulnerable, although in some areas the numbers are still critically low.

8. IRANIAN WOLF (*Canis lupus pallipes*)

Identified as a gray wolf subspecies in 1931 by English naturalist William Henry Sykes, the Iranian wolf had long been confused with the Indian wolf. However, Sykes's findings confirmed the Iranian wolf was indeed a unique subspecies.

The historic range of this wolf once covered all of southwest Asia and the Middle East. Today, it can be found in pockets in Israel, Iran, Turkey, and India. Its habitat consists of varied terrain, ranging from dense scrub forests to arid desert regions.

The Iranian wolf is quite small, measuring only 3 feet long and weighing less than 70 pounds. Its brown fur has a reddish tinge to it.

LEFT & ABOVE: The Italian wolf inhabits the Apennine Mountains and the western Alps.

At times it can be even mistaken for a fox. Coming from a hot and arid region of the world, this wolf's coat is made up of short, lightly colored, often gray fur and to prevent it overheating, it has little undercoat. Its ears are large to assist it in keeping cool. Interestingly, Iranian wolves are seldom heard howling. While it is not definitely known why they are so quiet, it is likely that it is due to the fact that they are simply not as protective of their territorial ranges as other wolves.

Although they live in packs of up to 15 individuals, Iranian wolves often hunt alone. Their main diet consists of rabbits, rodents, birds, and hares, most of which can be caught without the aid of other pack members.

Today, there are roughly 2,000 Iranian wolves left in the wild. Recently, there have been efforts by various organizations to find a way to preserve this beautiful wolf. Researchers understand, however, that in order to prevent this subspecies from becoming extinct, it will be necessary that villagers and livestock owners, who share the domain of this wolf, are educated about the conservation it.

9. ITALIAN WOLF (*Canis lupus italicus*)

Also known as the Apennine wolf, there is dispute as to whether or not the Italian wolf is a subspecies of gray wolf or a separate species of its own. In 1921, the Italian zoologist Joseph Altobello first described the Italian wolf, but it wasn't until 1999 that it was officially classified as a subspecies of gray wolf. Since then however, there has been renewed controversy about its classification.

ABOVE & RIGHT: The tundra wolf generally resides in river valleys, thickets, and forest clearings. In winter, it feeds almost exclusively on female or young, wild or domestic reindeer. It will also prey on hares, arctic foxes, and other smaller animals.

The Italian wolf lives chiefly in the Apennine Mountains in Italy. Now protected, their numbers are improving and as a consequence there have been reports of sightings in other parts of Italy, the south of France, and Switzerland. Historically, the Italian wolf ranged throughout these countries and many other European countries, too.

This medium-sized subspecies is slightly less than five feet in length. While females are roughly ten percent smaller than males, the average weight is between 50 and 90 pounds. The Italian wolf's coat is often a blend of brown and gray, although some have been found to be entirely black.

Known to hunt at night, Italian wolves feed primarily on medium and small mammals. For instance, they will eat rabbits, elk, red deer, wild boar, hares, chamois, and roe deer. They use plants, berries, and herbs as a source of fiber and in areas of human encroachment they feed on domestic pets, livestock, and even garbage.

Wolf populations in much of Italy and throughout the alpine region were almost completely annihilated by the end of the 1920s. Fierce persecution led to a severe reduction in the Italian wolf population in the Apennine regions as well.

In the early 1970s, two researchers launched a study of the Italian wolf in the Abruzzo Mountains, east of Rome. This brought the plight of the Italian wolf to the attention of the World Conservation Union who formally classified it as endangered. This intervention came just as the Italian wolf headed towards extinction. It is now estimated that their population is growing by seven percent annually. Today, there are roughly between 1,500 and 2,000 Italian wolves left in the wild.

10. TUNDRA WOLF (*Canis lupus albus*)

One of the largest of the wolves, the tundra wolf was classified as a subspecies of gray wolf in 1972 by Dr. Robert Kerr, a Scottish surgeon. The tundra wolf is a native of the boreal forests of Russia and Scandinavia and the high arctic. The tundra wolf can reach lengths of up to seven feet from tip to tip. They are an average of 3 feet tall and weigh between 100 and 125 pounds. However, there are unproven claims that some individuals can weigh as much as 220 pounds.

The tundra wolf has a striking silver-gray coat that can be tinged with black, and rust. Unfortunately, for the tundra wolf in the past, it was often hunted for its famously beautiful dense fur.

As with other large wolves, the tundra wolf preys first and foremost on large mammals. These include mountain sheep, deer, musk ox, wapiti, bison, moose, and caribou.

Loggers, hunters, and farmers are the tundra wolf's staunchest enemies and in some arctic islands they have been completely eradicated by hunters. However, in some other areas however, they are making a limited comeback and for this reason, the subspecies has been taken off some endangered lists.

THE RED WOLF (*Canis rufus*)

The red wolf is believed to be the only surviving wolf that evolved in North America. The noted naturalists, John Bachman and John Audubon originally identified *Canis rufus* as a distinct species of wolf in 1851. Nevertheless, biologists today still dispute whether the red wolf is a true wolf species or a hybrid result from interbreeding between coyotes and gray wolves. It is important to note that there is no genetic evidence to support this position.

A closer look at the red wolf shows a truly unique and beautiful animal that has a key role in our natural world.

BELOW & OVERLEAF: Red wolves may have been the first New World wolf species to be encountered by European colonists. They were originally distributed throughout the eastern United States from the Atlantic Ocean to central Texas. To the north they lived in a region from the Ohio River Valley to northern Pennsylvania and from New York south to the Gulf of Mexico.

WOLF SPECIES: PAST & PRESENT

PHYSICAL CHARACTERISTICS

It is easy to understand why some may think that the red wolf is merely a hybrid of the gray wolf the and coyote. While the red wolf does resemble a coyote in many ways, it is considerably larger like a gray wolf. When compared to its cousin the gray wolf, the red wolf's physique is more slender and shorter in stature. Moreover, its muzzle is longer and sharper due to an elongated head, much like that of a coyote. Conversely, when compared to a coyote, the red wolf dominates in size by quite a bit. Its frame is considerably more stout and solid. Furthermore, the legs of the red wolf are longer and the ears larger. The coat of the red wolf is what drives the coyote hybrid theory the most. Rather like a coyote, the red wolf can be tawny, light brown or tan in color. However, the majority of this species is mostly reddish-brown. On rare occasions the red wolf can be black.

The red wolf's coat is shorter and coarser than that of its cousin, the gray wolf. It has a long fluffy tail of about a foot in length and has strong legs which make it a fast runner. Interestingly, the red wolf is faster than the gray wolf.

The size of the red wolf depends on the availability of prey, the health of the pack line, and the range available. On average, a red wolf is just over two feet tall at the shoulder and about five feet long from tip to tip (the tip of the nose to the tip of the tail). A typical red wolf weighs 65 pounds on average.

HABITAT & TERRITORY

The red wolf is well-suited to a multitude of environments. Thus, it can live in a wide variety of different habitats including forests, coastal prairies, and even swamps. However, with the vast historic range that was attributed to the red wolf, it is likely most habitats would be acceptable to it. In fact, anywhere that prey populations are sufficient and human interference and persecution is minimal is a good habitat for the red wolf.

The historic range of the red wolf has been debated and expanded several times. Initial demarcations of their range were deemed too limiting and narrow. Considering that by the time scientific surveys of this range began it had already been brutally reduced.

In 1979, when the surveys began, researchers believed that the historical distribution was limited to the southeastern United States. Skeletal remains, foot prints, and other evidence pointed scientists to expand the range in 1995 north into central Pennsylvania. By 2002, the historical range was redefined again to extend farther north into the northeastern United States and even into the far eastern edge of Canada.

Recent genetic evidence suggests a much larger expansion to the historic range of the red wolf. So today, it is now believed that this ruddy canid once traversed a vast expanse of the eastern United States. This range ran from the Atlantic Ocean to the Edwards Plateau in Texas and from the Gulf of Mexico in the south, northward into the Algonquin Provincial Park in the south of Ontario in Canada.

In contrast to this enormous historic range, one of the only places that red wolves exist today is in North Carolina's Alligator River National Wildlife Refuge. The only other locations where red wolves can be found are in several zoos that participate in captive breeding programs.

The Alligator River National Wildlife Refuge is unique because it is home to the only wild population of red wolves in the world. These were reintroduced into the park with the hope they could adapt to a wild state. Here, they are shielded and protected from hazards. The area of North Carolina, where these red wolves live, is an area of forest and brush that provides adequate cover for them. Moreover, the reintroduced wolves have adapted and utilized the habitats available. In particular, the red wolves here inhabit pocosins which are a type of acidic wetland and forested area. In the pocosins, the wolves can find ample ground and canopy cover and can live in relative peace. While pocosins are not the best environment for red wolves, they have managed adapt to the conditions there.

Unfortunately, for the red wolf, recent studies show that the red wolves at Alligator River National Wildlife Refuge are not doing as well as they should be. In 2006, there were 130 wolves in the park. However, since then, the number of wolves has declined to 40, with further decline expected. Gunshot wounds and traffic collisions have contributed to their mortality. Meanwhile, breeding with coyotes looms as a threat to their genetic distinctiveness.

PACK LIFE & REPRODUCTION

As with most wolves, the red wolf lives in a familial pack. The pack is usually made up of less than ten individuals including the alpha pair. While a pack does not always need to hunt together, individuals will use pack behavior to protect their home range against intruders.

By nature, red wolves are not as territorial as their gray wolf cousins. It has been observed that they have the ability to pass within sight of another pack without an all-out war starting. This is possibly be due to the fact that neighboring packs comprise close relatives and therefore, individuals recognize each other.

The alpha pair lead the pack and are the only wolves in the pack that mate. Like other wolves, the red wolf alphas are pair bonded and raise their pups together.

The mating season falls in mid to late winter, usually between February and March. Pregnant alphas and their mates will find and set up birthing dens during the gestation period before the pups are born. These birthing dens are built in areas of dense vegetation, in hollowed

trees or logs, in sandy knolls, or in abandoned dens of other animals. Sometimes, they are built along the banks of creeks, streams, or rivers.

In mid to late Spring, the mother red wolf will give birth to a litter of between two and eight pups, although four or five are the average. Both alphas actively participate in the raising and protection of the young pups. Red wolf pups are born blind and deaf like their gray wolf cousins. They remain in the den with their mother, nursing every couple of hours for the first month of their lives. After that, the mother leaves the den to hunt and help patrol the territory. She returns every

LEFT & BELOW: The red wolf is considered to be the rarest species of wolf and the most endangered in the world.

few hours to further nurse the pups until they are old enough to be weaned and leave the den, usually at about six to eight weeks of age. However, the pups are never left alone while in the den. The parents and other pack members share the job of caring for their youngest members.

Once weaned, the pups will join the rest of the pack and begin eating meat provided by the father and other pack members. This will carry on until they are old enough to fend for themselves. Red wolves reach sexual maturity when they are roughly two years of age. At this point, the young wolves will often leave their birth pack to venture out into the world and start their own.

Thus, every two to four years the pack changes. Unlike gray wolves, the red wolf does not have a litter of pups every year. Often

the alphas will not mate again until their last litter of pups have grown and left the pack. This lends a year on, year off type rhythm to the mating cycle of the red wolf, with new litters born to replace those pack members that are leaving to start their own families/packs.

Red wolves are shy and secretive animals that often live in pack territories that average 50 square miles in size. They live for six to seven years in the wild and up to 15 years in captivity. With so few red wolves left in the wild, it is difficult to assess statistics. However, their short life expectancy in the wild is likely to be attributable to human persecution and interference, combined with starvation due to depletion of prey populations.

DIET & HUNTING

Red wolves subsist on a wide and varied diet that depends largely on what is available in their territory. The red wolf is a competent predator. Generally speaking, it is a nocturnal hunter that uses its sharp senses and stealth to track down its prey. It eats on average between two to five pounds of food each day.

The alpha pair may occasionally hunt and bring down young white-tailed deer when they are available. However, they more often hunt for smaller game such as small mammals including rabbits, raccoons, hares, and small rodents such as squirrels, mice, weasels, and the American marten. Other than grouse and prairie chickens, the wild red wolf seldom feeds on birds, but will if its preferred source of meat is limited or absent. Furthermore, the red wolf will scavenge for carrion and on occasions has been known to kill and eat domestic pets and livestock. The red wolf is often a lone hunter. This is because its prey tends to be small animals that do not need bringing down by a pack.

Red wolves are consummate nocturnal hunters and nature has given them all the tools they need. Their senses of smell, sight, and hearing are as finely attuned as those of their cousin the gray wolf. This means that their senses can vastly outdo anything a human can manage. The red wolf can see for over three miles in an open space. Its ears can pick up sounds from over ten miles away. They are able to follow a scent trail for dozens of miles and across all terrains other than water.

ADAPTATIONS

When compared to the gray wolf, the red wolf has several adapations that are exclusive the this species.

Historically, red wolves live in areas with uneven, rocky terrain. In order for the animal to hunt and survive in those areas their toes have been adapted to give them better traction. This adaptation allows them to maintain higher speeds when running and better balance.

The red wolf walks on its toes rather than its whole foot. This adaptation allows it to launch into pursuit or flight at a moment's

notice. It is also faster than its gray wolf cousin. This stance also allows it to step lightly and silently when stalking its prey through the darkened landscape of its home territory.

During winter months when the night temperatures are uncomfortably low, the red wolf can alter its nocturnal habit by hunting at dawn and dusk and more throughout the day.

Another major adaptation that the red wolf has undergone, is the ability to live in the southeastern United States; known for its hot summers. The red wolf goes through a seasonal molt in the spring in order to shed off its heavy winter coat. The summer coat is lighter and cooler. Another key adaptation of the red wolf that helps it to keep itself cool in the hot southern summers, is its large ears. Wider and taller than those of the gray wolf, the ears of the red wolf often seem too big for its head. Nevertheless, its larger ears allow body heat to escape due to the large surface area of them.

A further adaptation that has allowed the red wolf to survive when other canines have not been so lucky is currently fascinating scientists. This adaptation allows the red wolf to survive an infestation of heart worm.

Heart worm is a lethal parasite that often enters the body of wolves through mosquito bites. Since it is impossible to prevent mosquitos from biting the red wolf in the southeastern United States, this adaptation was essential for survival. These 12-inch worms will attach themselves to the heart, lungs, and associated blood vessels of their host and cut off the ability of that organ to function causing heart failure, lung disease, and other organ damage.

The adaptation of the red wolf that has researchers so excited does not prevent them from getting heart worm but rather somehow prevents the parasite from killing them. Researchers have conducted several tests to determine how many of the red wolves that were released into the wild for reintroduction efforts have heart worm. Every single one of the wolves tested had the parasite which is vastly higher than the average infection rate of under two percent in domestic dogs.

Further, untreated heartworm in domestic dogs has a 98 percent mortality rate. That means that nearly every dog that gets heartworm and has it go untreated will die from those parasitic worms. However, research showed that although 100 percent of the red wolf population was infected only ten percent of those infected wolves died from conditions that could be tied to the worms.

Somehow, the red wolf has developed the ability to resist the deadly effects of the heartworm.

STATUS & CONSERVATION

In the last hundred years, the human population has grown exponentially and as a result the natural habitats of many of our plant and animals species have been reduced or destroyed. The destruction of natural prey populations and the addition of livestock farming has led to constant conflict between man and the natural world. This conflict has been particularly devastating for the red wolf. To man, the red wolf was nothing more than a nuisance.

Predator control programs were enacted that encouraged the hunting, trapping, and poisoning of wolves. Posters declaring "The only good wolf is a dead wolf" were a common sight in the early twentieth century. Due to this attitude and campaign, the red wolf was entirely annihilated in the eastern portion of their historic range in the first twenty years of the last century.

Continued programs, including federally sponsored campaigns against the red wolf continued throughout the 1960s and into the 1970s. Efforts by the Endangered Species Act in the mid-70s were too

BELOW: The red wolf has larger ears than the gray wolf.

little, too late and by 1980, the red wolf was persecuted to the point of extinction in the wild. It was only when they were almost gone that scientists realized how important the red wolf was to the environment and North America's natural heritage.

The red wolf is now identified as a keystone species and an apex predator. Both of these labels indicate a species that is essential to the survival of the global ecosystem. A keystone species is defined as a species that other species within an ecosystem depend upon, to the extent that if that species were removed, the entire ecosystem would be drastically changed.

An apex predator is a creature that is at the top of the food chain and has no natural predators. While the populations of these predators need to be controlled, their loss creates a cataclysmic domino effect within an ecosystem. If the main predator of an area is removed, then the prey populations that they feed on will grow unchecked. This leads to overpopulation which then leads to resource depletion including disease and starvation. Like the loss of a keystone species, the loss of an apex predator leads to the eventual collapse of the entire ecosystem.

With this understanding came the creation of captive breeding programs in the 1970s in which areas all across the United States took part. To facilitate this, 40 red wolves were captured in the late 1970s for genetic testing. Fourteen of those 40 individuals were found to be genetically pure specimens of red wolf and those were the ones then used for captive breeding.

In 1987 the first red wolves were released back into the wild. This historic occasion marked the first time an animal had been brought back from extinction in the wild. This set the stage for many of the captive breeding programs that followed for the red wolf's gray cousin.

The area in North Carolina that was considered ideal for this reintroduction was chosen in part because of its complete lack of a coyote population. At the time, it was considered very important that hybridization with coyotes didn't happen. The United States Fish and Wildlife Service, who were in charge of the reintroduction effort, wanted to avoid that problem. Unfortunately, in the 1990s the coyote population of this area unexpectedly grew and became well established. Today, hybridization is still a significant problem for the red wolves in this area.

Human induced red wolf mortality continues to be a problem, predominantly in the form of car accidents. However, humans have shot red wolves since their reintroduction despite the fact that they are listed as critically endangered. To deliberately kill a red wolf is a federal offense. Today, in North Carolina, red wolf numbers are worryingly low.

RED WOLF SUBSPECIES

There were only two subspecies of red wolf ever known to have existed. They are *Canis rufus floridanus* and *Canis rufus gregoryi*—both of which are now extinct.

GREGORY'S WOLF (*Canis rufus gregoryi*)

This subspecies of the red wolf was commonly known as Gregory's wolf, the Mississippi Valley wolf, the Texas red wolf, and even the swamp wolf. It resided in a historical range that included regions in and around the lower Mississippi River basin.

Taller than the standard red wolf, this subspecies was slenderer in frame. Its coat was a blend of black, gray, and white. It had a generous streak of bright red running from the top of its head and down its back. They weighed roughly 65 pounds on average and were considered by some to be a genetic bridge between true red wolves and the other subspecies of red wolf, the Florida black wolf.

FLORIDA BLACK WOLF (*Canis rufus floridanus*)

The Florida black wolf, as its name suggests, was found throughout the majority of central and northern Florida and the border areas surrounding it. It was larger than the red wolf both in height and length. This may be what led to the previously held belief that this wolf was actually a subspecies of gray wolf rather than red. Genetic testing proved this false however.

As their name suggests, this wolf had a distinctive jet-black coat that was unusual and unique. They were driven to extinction by 1908 through human encroachment, habitat destruction, and predator reduction efforts which included poisoning, trapping, and hunting.

ABYSSINIAN WOLF (*Canis simensis*)

For decades, the Abyssinian wolf, also known as the Ethiopian wolf, was denied its true heritage. When DNA testing was finally done on what was then known as the Ethiopian jackal, it was found to be more closely related to the gray wolf than any other African canine. Thus, *Canis simensis* garnered the classification of the third species of wolf in the world.

This overlooked wolf is known by many names. In addition to Abyssinian wolf and Ethiopian wolf, it is also known as Simien fox, Simien jackal, and red fox. Furthermore, in the Amharic, the official language of Ethiopia, it is called *ky kebero* which translates to red jackal. Similarly, in the regional language of the African Horn, Afan Oromo, it is called the *jeedala fardaa* (horse's jackal).

PHYSICAL DESCRIPTION

Based on the appearance of the Abyssinian wolf, the confusion over this small wolf's taxonomy (the branch of science that deals with the classification of animals) is understandable. These African wolves look more like a large fox or jackal than a small wolf. However, DNA does not lie.

Abyssinian wolves are much smaller than a jackal. It is on average, 4 feet long from the tip of its nose to tip of its tail, 2 feet tall and weighs roughly 30 to 40 pounds. It has broad pointed ears and a long, pointed snout. Furthermore, its distinctive reddish coat is suggestive of a fox or a red wolf, rather than a gray wolf that it is more closely related to. In addition to the red coloring, its coat often has white patches on their underparts, chest, and throat. Their tail is long, bushy, and black with a white base.

BELOW: An Abyssinian wolf on the Sanetti Plateau in the Bale Mountains in Ethiopia.

HABITAT & TERRITORY

The Abyssinian wolf lives at altitudes of roughly 10,000 feet in the mountains regions of southern and northern Ethiopia. The heathlands and grasslands of this region provide the ideal habitat for this small wolf. The Abyssinian wolf has a relatively small territory comprising three square miles in area on average.

The Bale Mountain National Park boasts the largest population of Abyssinian wolves in Africa, moreover, in the world. In fact, this concentration this interesting wolf represents more than half of the total population of Abyssinian wolves.

BEHAVIOR

Like all wolves, Abyssinian wolves are social animals that form packs. These packs work cooperatively to patrol their territory three times

daily, in the early mornings, at noon, and in the evening. However, for the rest of the day they are solitary foragers. Hunting is naturally a daytime activity for the Abyssinian wolf, however, in areas where they are persecuted they have been known to go against their nature and become nocturnal hunters.

Furthermore, this is one of the only animals that can form associations with other species to catch their prey. For the Abyssinian wolf this cohort is the gelada, a primate found exclusively in the Ethiopian highlands.

Abyssinian wolves are much less aggressive than other wolves. This is true both within their own pack as well as when confronted by another pack.

MATING & REPRODUCTION

As with other wolves, only the alpha pair breed in Abyssinian wolf packs. Mating during the months of August through November, litters are produced between October and January. During the breeding season and pregnancy, a female Abyssinian wolf's coat will turn a pale yellow color while her tail loses hair and that which remains lightens to brown.

When young female members of the pack reach sexual maturity, they venture off to find a new pack. This is a biological safeguard against inbreeding which weakens both the individuals and the pack as a whole.

COMMUNICATION

These wolves have a vast assortment of vocalization in their communication repertoire. Greetings involve high-frequency whines to demonstrate submission or growls as a cautionary threat. When sounding the alarm, the Abyssinian wolf will huff before moving into yelps and barks. At pack gatherings, they will participate in a group yip-howl that can be heard from three miles away.

DIET

The Abyssinian wolf's diet is 90 percent rodents. If their prey is underground they dig out their prey with their small paws and long snout. In rare instances, they form a pack to hunt larger animals including lambs, hares, and even small antelopes.

ADAPTATIONS

The Abyssinian wolf has an unusually narrow muzzle that helps it to get into the burrows of the rodents and other small prey it hunts.

Widely spaced teeth help them to tear, grind, and devour meat with little difficulty.

STATUS

The Abyssinian wolf is the second most endangered species of wolf in the world, with the Red wolf taking first. For the first time, humans are not the biggest threat to a species of wolf. A recurring rabies epidemic that is transmitted through other wolves and domestic dogs is the biggest threat to the Abyssinian wolf. There are an estimated 500 Abyssinian wolves in the wild and none in captivity. A rigorous conservation effort with a straightforward plan of action has been undertaken to stop the extinction of this unique wolf. In addition, it is protected by Ethiopian law.

SUBSPECIES

There were two recognized subspecies of the Abyssinian wolf, both of which are extinct.

LEFT & RIGHT: The Abyssinian wolf is much smaller than the other wolf species. They mainly eat small rodents.

WOLVES THROUGHOUT THE SEASONS

CHAPTER FOUR
WOLVES THROUGHOUT
THE SEASONS

Wolves live in almost every environment around the globe from the frozen lands of the north to the desert wildernesses further south. They also inhabit wetlands, swamps, forests, mountainous regions, and almost every other habitat in between. Wherever they are located; how they reproduce, hunt, and live their lives, will be influenced by the variation in the seasons. Therefore, it stands to reason that wolves living in the colder climes will have a markedly

BELOW: Three handsome members of an eastern timber wolf pack.

RIGHT: The Arctic wolf is one of the most striking of all the gray wolf subspecies.

OVERLEAF: An alpha male and an alpha female in their home territory.

different way of life to those wolves living in desert regions. Despite this, there will always be some generalities that will apply to all wolves the whole world over. Our story begins in winter.

"A wolf pup's first year can be very difficult. While the population about doubles when pups are born, about 70 percent will die in their first year due to starvation, drowning, accidents, disease, predators, and human causes."
~ Dr. L. David Mech, vice chair and founder of the International Wolf Center.

WINTER

The days grow shorter and the winds colder. Soon a blanket of snow covers everything and warmth is something that is hard to find. Winter is a time of death and sleep, but for the wolf it is a time of resurgence.

The wolf pack is in its prime in the winter months. At this time, pack numbers are at their highest and all members are ready for a season of hunting. Their stomachs are empty.

In winter, the wolf's inner layer of fur thickens to keep it waterproof and warm. The outer layer thickens as well, to provide further protection from the extreme cold. This thick double-layering keeps the wolf warm even on the coldest of winter night. In fact, the wolf is so insulated that little or no body heat can escape through its coat and sometimes, to prove this theory, when snow lands on a wolf's back it will not melt. On frigid winter nights, wolves will huddle together for warmth and fall asleep close to their pack mates for

BELOW & OPPOSITE: During the winter months in the frozen north, the wolf's beautiful, dense, and luxurious coat protects it from the extreme temperatures that can prevail for months on end.

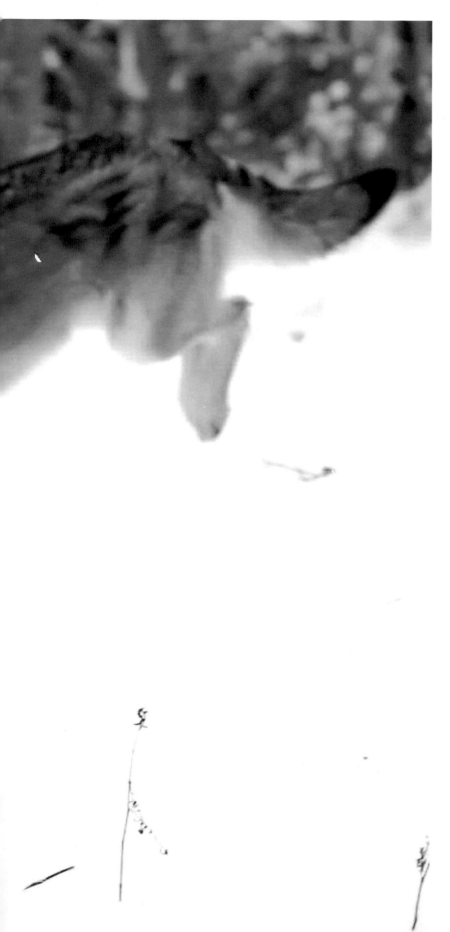

added warmth. They curl their vulnerable feet up close to their bodies and tuck their noses in under their bushy tails. This way of sleeping is quite resourceful and serves more than one purpose. The wolf's exhaled breath helps to keep its feet and nose warm and furthermore, when the wolf breathes in, the air it takes will be already warmed by the wolf's tail fur.

HUNTING

In winter, wolves have a decided advantage over the large hoofed herbivores that most of them prefer to hunt and eat. The wide feet of the wolf act like snowshoes. This allows them to travel faster and farther on the surface of the crusty snow. Their prey, however, are less well adapted and are slowed down by the deep snowy conditions. In fact, for the wolf's prey, wintertime is a season of difficulty and hardship. When hunting, it is usual for a wolf pack to travel up to 40

LEFT & ABOVE: Wolves find it easier to hunt in winter as their prey is often more visible and sometimes slower and weaker.

miles per day in pursuit. In order to make things easier for them, they usually prefer to hunt the weak, old, or sick. Their main prey in the frozen north include large herbivores such as deer, elk, moose, bison, bighorn sheep, caribou, and musk oxen. Despite being highly skilled, this prolific hunter still needs to conserve as much of their energy as possible. Their technique for this, is to stay upwind and out of sight for as long as possible. The wolves will then follow a trail left by the animal they are stalking. When the opportune moment presents itself, or they are spotted by their prey, they will give chase.

Often, the young wolves born in the past spring are on their first proper hunt at this time of year. This is a time for them to watch, learn, and perfect their hunting techniques for the future. Sometimes, however, the older wolves find it difficult to control the pups' excitement and occasionally a hunt can be ruined when an over-enthusiastic pup takes chase too early.

During this time of plenty, the wolf gains weight and condition. It also achieves a high degree of fitness and stamina, and providing that the wolf's food source continues, all members of the pack will be well-prepared for the mating season and the birth of their pups in early spring.

MATING

In the frozen lands of the north, winter is the season for mating. The female wolf usually goes into heat in late-December or early-January. This is the time when the alpha pair begin their courtship. The courtship is a week long affair that ends with repeated copulation.

LEFT, BELOW & OVERLEAF: Alpha pairs, pictured here, are usually the only ones in the pack allowed to breed.

Once the female alpha is pregnant she will gestate for 63 days, which is usually the remainder of the winter. She hunts with the rest of the pack for the entire period of her pregnancy. Alpha mothers are warriors who slow down for nothing.

At the end of the long dark winter, the cold and ice give way to the beginning of spring. At this time, the snow starts to melt and the fierce icy winds turn into gentle breezes. As the days become longer and balmier, the wolves have more time to follow the herds, socialize with each other, and even play together.

BELOW & RIGHT: The arrival of spring in British Columbia, Canada. These young gray wolves are enjoying the warmer weather the new season brings.

OVERLEAF: This pregnant Arctic wolf is ready to give birth.

LEFT & BELOW: The alpha female wolf usually chooses the den in which to give birth. However, it is the rest of the pack who prepare it for her by digging out a hollow.

SPRING

Springtime in the Arctic is all about babies!

Despite the short growing season, spring in the Arctic is a beautiful sight when all the flowers seem to bloom at once. The trees also seem to come into bud almost overnight. As the sun gains strength, all the plants and animals become invigorated with new energy and purpose. The time has come again, for new life to begin in the wolf pack.

LEFT, BELOW & OVERLEAF: When wolf pups are young, they hone their life skills by exploring and play fighting. This is always done under the watchful eyes of other adult pack members.

By very early spring, the alpha female will be already pregnant. For this reason, it is essential that time is spent preparing the den for the arrival of the new pups. The female will choose an appropriate site for the den and then supervise the building or remodeling of it. The alpha male and the rest of the pack will help with the task.

The female chooses a den that is easily defendable, has access to water, and provides protection from the elements. The den is usually made from hollowed out logs or trees, crevices in rocky areas, abandoned beaver lodges, or even small caverns dug out of the ground.

Later on in the spring, the pups arrive. At this time, they are deaf, blind and totally defenseless. The litter will comprise of somewhere between two and ten pups, but the average litter size is four to eight. Their mother spends the first three to four weeks in the den nursing them. At this time, the alpha male and other pack members will bring the female food and guard the den. As the pups grow and become stronger, the female is able to leave the den for brief periods, but when she does, other members of the pack will keep watch.

The pups stumble out into the world at roughly two to three months old. By this time, they will be able to eat solid food. The den is then abandoned. The female then relocates the pups to a "rendezvous site." This is a more open area, away from the original den, but closer to where the adults hunt. When at the rendezvous site, the pups exercise and build up their strength playing. They particularly enjoy wrestling, tag, and hide and seek. These games help to develop the skills these young wolves will need as adults. They also spend time here bonding with the other members of their pack/family.

The wolf is a highly social animal and therefore, each new pup will have its own personality and its own strengths and weaknesses. How it interacts with its siblings and other pack members at this early stage of life will pave the way for its future role in the pack. Ultimately, the pups who are the healthiest, the most dominant, and the most gregarious will eventually become full-fledged members of

ABOVE: Young wolves learn life skills by copying the behavior of other pack members. This pup is learning how to pick up a scent.

RIGHT & OVERLEAF: As the pups grow in size, so does their independence and confidence.

their pack. Docile submissive pups, however, might have a future as a subordinate or even an omega (a wolf at the bottom of the hierarchy). On the other hand, those pups that show high levels of aggression and independence are more likely to leave the pack when ready and start a new one as an alpha.

Understandably, raising young pups during the springtime is very labor-intensive. As a consequence, the pack reduces the amount of

212

time it spends hunting and following the herds during this period. The warmer temperatures too, mean that the pack can be less preoccupied with the constant drive for food that the winter dictates. However, despite these easier times, the pack still has to eat. This is also the time of year when other young are born, including white-tailed deer. The fawns are easy prey to a pack of hungry wolves.

For the wolf pack, the heady days of spring are over more than too quickly, so before long, summer arrives.

SUMMER

As the days get longer and warmer, the wolf pack becomes less active during the hottest part of the day. They limit themselves to their nocturnal habit of hunting in the evening or at night.

The pups have spent the spring and summer growing rapidly and learning the skills required for adult life. By the end of the summer, some of them will be six to eight months old and some will have learned to hunt, although most will be observers and not quite ready to

LEFT & ABOVE: Wolf pups grow rapidly throughout the summer and it is at this time that they learn how to howl and how to use other vocal skills. It is also a time of play and exploration.

make a kill themselves. By now their teeth and digestion are strong enough to feed on a kill alongside the other pack members.

Unfortunately, for the pack, summer can be a difficult time for it is when the most conflicts occur between neighboring packs. When a pack tracks its prey, it is easy for it to wander into another's territory. It is not uncommon for fierce fighting to break out between the rival packs. Sadly, the fighting can be so prolonged and vicious that some pack members may be badly wounded or in some cases killed.

217

AUTUMN

Too soon the long days of summer begin to fade into the cooler days of the fall. The trees and shrubs are covered in colorful berries. It is a time of plenty for the mammals and birds which feed on them. As the days grow shorter and the nights longer, the wolves are stirring, for the a new season brings change.

When the leaves start to fall from the trees, and the once dazzling sun becomes a golden haze, the wolves must prepare for winter. At this time, the wolf's coat is changing. Before long, it becomes thicker,

BELOW: For the young female Eurasian gray wolf, this will be her first winter.

RIGHT: The fall is a particularly beautiful time of year and it can be easy to forget that winter is just around the corner. However, at this time, the Arctic wolf has already grown a dense coat in preparation for the winter to come.

OVERLEAF: A handsome gray wolf in the fall.

heavier, and more luxurious. It takes about three weeks for a wolf to change its coat and during this time, it can look quite scruffy and patchy. Wolves who live in the highest latitudes have the heaviest coats in winter. In contrast, wolves who live farther south tend to grow much thinner coats in winter.

Once the great herds of herbivores start to head off to their winter grazing grounds, the pack starts to become restless, for it is time for them to follow. The pack can only survive if it stays close to its prey. Despite this, a wolf pack will only follow a herd to the edge of its own territory. It will not venture out of it.

By now, the young wolves are about 50 pounds in weight and are still growing fast. They will now be hunting and learning how to survive without the constant support of a parent. This is also a time

that the older pups of around two years of age will have reached sexual maturity. Some will disperse from the pack, a strategy that gives them time to start pairing up and form their own pack.

Towards the end of the fall, the bad weather starts to set in and the wolves sense this change in the seasons. The wolves are prepared, fit, and ready for the challenge of winter.

BELOW & RIGHT: As winter approaches, the wolf pack will be on the move. It is time to follow the herds.

WORLDWIDE
WOLF CONSERVATION

CHAPTER FIVE
WORLDWIDE
WOLF CONSERVATION

Throughout the world, wolves of every species and subspecies have been persecuted, hunted, vilified, and unfairly treated in a multitude of ways. The expansion of the human population and its subsequent occupation of new lands, has meant that the wolf, who had previously lived undisturbed for thousands of years, was now coming into conflict with the new arrivals. Entire governments waged war against the wolf, an animal that had committed no crime. All the wolf wanted to do was to survive. Called monster, villain, fiend, and many other derogatory names, the wolf was reviled in history, image, and myth. It bears consideration though, that while not one healthy wolf has ever attacked a human; humans have trapped, poisoned, and hunted them, almost causing their worldwide extinction.

"For almost two centuries, American gray wolves, vilified in fact as well as fiction, were the victims of vicious government extermination programs. By the time the Endangered Species Act was passed in 1973, only a few hundred of these once-great predators were left in the lower 48 states."
~ Lydia Millet, American author and Pulitzer Prize finalist.

BELOW, RIGHT & OVERLEAF: The wolf is without a doubt one of the most beautiful animals on the planet. Sadly, it has also been one of the most persecuted.

Up until the 1970s, little regard had been given to the wolf's plight. In fact, many countries still permitted hunting it. Most species and subspecies of wolf hadn't even made it onto an endangered species list. However, as time went on, nature conservation in general, gained momentum and started to feature more heavily in politics. The general public too, were starting to understand the need to protect our natural resources including animal and plant species as well as their habitats for the future.

BELOW & RIGHT: Both of the wolves pictured here are part of a conservation program in Yellowstone National Park.

OVERLEAF: A gray wolf in Kootenay National Park in Canada.

WORLDWIDE WOLF CONSERVATION

Scientists were also on the case as well. They started to undertake more complex studies of the natural world including how ecosystems worked, the importance of predator-prey relationships, and how important it was to conserve the natural environment as a whole. With so many extinctions that had occurred in the previous hundred years or so, it was suddenly apparent that if a species was lost, it was lost for good.

The wolf has been identified as a keystone species which is a species that is important to the ecosystem it lives in. Usually, a keystone species is a predator, but not always. Furthermore, the wolf is also an apex predator which means it is at the top of the food chain and therefore, has no natural predators. In a well-balanced natural environment the number of apex predators is finely attuned to the number of its prey. However, in a situation where the main apex

predator is removed, the prey population that they feed on will grow unrestricted. This leads to the overpopulation of the prey species, ultimately resulting in disease and starvation.

Fortunately, for the last remaining populations of wolves around the world, the vast majority of governments now realize that the wolf urgently requires protection. Sadly though, there are still a few countries that consider the wolf a low priority in terms of its conservation. Some governments are not prepared to regulate how many wolves are killed by hunters and even worse, some governments actively promote the hunting wolves by offering bounties.

LEFT & BELOW: These gray wolves are now protected in Denali National Park and Preserve, Alaska.

Luckily for the wolf today, in most countries things have changed for the better. It is now widely understood how important the wolf is to the natural world and how vital it is that it has our protection. Governments, conservation groups, and other organizations are now working to repair the existing wolf populations around the globe.

WORLD WILDLIFE FUND
The WWF works tirelessly to conserve animal populations across the world. They are one of the best-known conservation groups and consequently, have a vast reach. This famous and charitable organization divides its resources among a plethora of conservation projects. Fortunately, saving our wolves is one of their most important programs.

The World Wildlife Fund's Symbolic Species Adoption program offers 140 different endangered and threatened species to "adopt." Their gray wolf package is one of the most popular. Gray wolf "adoption kits" range in price from $25 to $250. The money raised goes to the charity in general rather than directly to gray wolf conservation. However, the most important thing that this conservation group does for the wolf, is to draw attention to the human activities that threaten its existence in the wild. If the WWF is alerted to a corporation, government, or individual that may be endangering wolves, it will name and shame the offender/s through television or in newspapers and magazines.

BELOW: Due to great efforts in conservation and reintroducing animals into the wild again, wolf numbers in the United States are slowly rising.

RIGHT: These Eurasian gray wolves live in safety in a national park in Bavaria, Germany.

The WWF also organizes protests to promote its causes and can serve lawsuits on those who cause harm to wildlife. Most importantly for the wolf however, it publicizes and draws worldwide attention to the wolf's plight.

CENTER FOR BIOLOGICAL DIVERSITY

Founded in 1989 by three young surveyors for the United States Forest Service, the Center for Biological Diversity, or more simply The Center, is dedicated to saving the ecological systems of the world from collapse. The Center is a leader in endangered species conservation within the United States. It does this by securing legislation and recognition of the Endangered Species Act. It strives to protect hundreds of endangered species and habitats in several million acres of water and land.

The Center has a large database concerning wolf conservation and its recovery in the wild. It then uses this data to prioritize intervention where necessary. In some cases The Center has filed lawsuits to force federal protections for endangered species. Moreover, The Center also serves as a watchdog for governmental agencies to ensure that sound conservation policy is being created and followed.

Since its formation, The Center has accomplished the following;
- Defeated aggressive attempts by conservative lawmakers to undermine the Endangered Species Act by supplying sound science and statistical analysis to policymakers.
- •. Won a landmark settlement that compelled the US Fish and Wildlife Service to declare protection status for several sub species of gray wolf and the red wolf. It also has protected hundreds of other endangered species.

The Center also supports the following conservation groups:
- Wolf Conservation Center
- Earthjustice
- Natural Resources Defense Council
- Sierra Club
- Predator Defense

ABOVE & RIGHT: The WWF are committed to the conservation of wolf species. Pictured right is the critically endangered red wolf.

- Pacific Wolf Coalition
- National Wolfwatcher Coalition
- local and regional organizations that conserve wolf species and other endangered species in general.

GOVERNMENT EFFORTS IN WOLF CONSERVATION
While the government of the United States has not always been the friend of the wolf, it has made efforts towards its conservation. The government has initiated programs to conserve and reintroduce the Mexican gray wolf, the red wolf, and the gray wolf. There have been some successes, but some failures, too.

RED WOLF CONSERVATION

Captive breeding programs were initiated in the 1970s across the United States. To facilitate this, 40 red wolves' were captured for genetic testing to determine their genetic purity. Only 14 of those 40 individuals were found to be genetically pure specimens. These were then used for the captive breeding programs.

The first red wolves were released back into the wild in 1987. This landmark event marked the first time any animal was brought back from extinction in the wild. It also set the stage for the gray wolf captive breeding programs that followed.

The area in North Carolina that was considered ideal for this reintroduction was chosen in part because of its complete lack of a coyote population. Hybridization with coyotes and coyote/wolf hybrids could potentially damage the remaining red wolves' genetic purity. The United States Fish and Wildlife Service were in charge of the reintroduction effort. Unfortunately, in the 1990s the coyote population of this area unexpectedly grew and became well established. This was a threat to the red wolf then, and is also a serious problem today. Human induced red wolf mortality continues to be a problem too, predominantly in the form of car accidents. However, and more worryingly, humans have shot red wolves since their reintroduction despite the fact that they are listed as critically endangered by the United States government.

Fewer than 40 red wolves exist in the wild today in the North Carolina reserve where they were introduced in the 1980s.

THE REINTRODUCTION TO YELLOWSTONE

In January of 1995, a white truck delivered eight gray wolves to the Yellowstone National Park. They were transported from Canada. Until then, they had not been seen in Yellowstone since the last pack was wiped out in the 1920s. The program continued and by the end of the second year, 31 gray wolves had been relocated to Yellowstone.

LEFT, ABOVE & PAGES: 242-243: The wolves in Yellowstone National Park were reintroduced in the 1990s.

Although there was resistance from some ranchers that owned land bordering the park, wildlife biologists persuaded the ranchers that the wolves were beneficial to the environment, by rebalancing the delicate ecosystem there. Previous to the introduction, the elk population had ballooned, wreaking havoc to the delicate vegetation in the park.

By 2014, there were 11 packs of gray wolves being tracked within the boundaries of Yellowstone National Park. While this is a success story to some degree, there are still some who are against having them in the park.

THE REINTRODUCTION TO IDAHO

At the same time that the gray wolf was reintroduced in Yellowstone, an effort was also underway to reintroduce them into central Idaho. This equally important conservation effort was vastly overshadowed by the more public Yellowstone reintroduction. Unfortunately, it was less successful, too. The Idaho reintroduction garnered less support from the conservation community. This was because wild wolves were beginning to migrate into Idaho from Canada naturally. They feared that introducing foreign wolves would stop this natural repopulation.

In addition, the release itself was problematic. Unlike the release in Yellowstone, which kept the animals penned for a time to adjust to their new surroundings, the Idaho reintroduction utilized a hard

release. A hard release meant that the animals were trapped in their home territory, transported thousands of miles, and then immediately released into an unfamiliar environment with no time for them to adjust to their new surroundings.

Unfortunately, the hard release didn't work too well. One female wolf from the first hard release in Idaho, traveled 60 miles in the first day, back towards her home range before being shot by a 74-year-old rancher. The wolf was eating the carcass of a stillborn calf. Others met similar fates as they wandered around the new landscape.

Despite this blundered beginning, things have worked out well in the end. At the end of 2017, the Idaho Department of Fish and Game reported 108 packs containing 786 gray wolves.

MEXICAN GRAY WOLF REINTRODUCTION

After the success of the Yellowstone and Idaho reintroductions, the US Fish and Wildlife Service tackled the extinct Mexican gray wolf. The last four individuals of the species were trapped in the mid-1970s to preserve the species. Three of these four were males and one was a female just entering mating age.

Following a captive breeding program, Mexican gray wolves were then released into parts of their historic home range in the mountains of southwestern Texas and Arizona in 1998. The area they were released in was deemed ideal for the animals to thrive in and was designated the Mexican Wolf Experimental Population Area (MWEPA).

WORLDWIDE WOLF CONSERVATION

LEFT, BELOW & OVERLEAF: With the help of a careful breeding program, the Mexican wolf was brought back from near extinction.

By the end of 2016, there were at least 113 Mexican gray wolves living and thriving within the MWEPA. That is more than a 16 percent increase from the year before and indicates a healthy, thriving population of Mexican gray wolves. As further proof of this, 65 pups were recorded as being born in 2015 with slightly less than 50 of those surviving to adulthood.

THE FUTURE OF THE WOLF

In order for the wolf to survive on this planet alongside man into the future, there has to be a concerted international effort to protect it. Despite some successes, the loss of habitat, reduction in prey species, and human-induced mortality are still the largest threats to their survival. Attitudes about wolves that stem from stories of "the big bad wolf" and sensational journalism may affect their survival even today.

The future is all about education, so that students, children, and adults alike can be educated to understand the history and plight of this wonderful animal.

"After numerous generations of people dedicated to killing wolves on the North American continent, one generation devoted itself to letting wolves live."
~ Lydia Millet, American novelist and Pulitzer Prize finalist.

RIGHT & OVERLEAF: Hopefully, humans have learned lessons from the past and will continue to let these beautiful creatures live in peace, free from persecution.

INDEX

BIBLIOGRAPHY

Dutcher, Jamie. *The Hidden Life of Wolves:*
National Geographic, 2009.
Dutcher, Jamie, and Jim Dutcher.. *The Wisdom of Wolves:*
Penguin Random House. 2018
Mech, David L. *Wolf: The Ecology and Behavior of an Endangered Species:*
The American Museum of Natural History/Doubleday, 1981.
Mech, David L. *Wolves: Behavior, Ecology, and Conservation:*
The University of Chicago Press, 2003.
Read, Tracy. C. *Exploring the World of Wolves:*
Firefly Books, 2010.
Beeland, DeLene T. *The Secret Life of Red Wolves*: T*he Fight to Save North America's Other Wolf:*
University of North Carolina Press, 2013.

ACKNOWLEDGEMENTS

All images have been supplied under license by © Shutterstock.com.

The copyright holder credits the following images as follows:
Page 214 left: Wiki Media Commons/Luis Garcia